THE *MAYFLOWER*

THE HISTORY SMASHERS SERIES

The Mayflower

Women's Right to Vote

THE *MAYFLOWER*

KATE MESSNER

ILLUSTRATED BY DYLAN MECONIS

With special thanks to Linda Coombs, an educator and historian from the
Aquinnah Wampanoag Tribe, who served as a consultant for this book

RANDOM HOUSE **NEW YORK**

Text copyright © 2020 by Kate Messner
Cover art and interior illustrations copyright © 2020 by Dylan Meconis

Visit us on the Web! rhcbooks.com

Educators and librarians, for a variety of teaching tools, visit us at RHTeachersLibrarians.com

Library of Congress Cataloging-in-Publication Data
Names: Messner, Kate, author. | Meconis, Dylan, illustrator.
Title: The Mayflower / Kate Messner; illustrated by Dylan Meconis.
Description: New York: Random House Children's Books, 2020. | Series:
History smashers | Includes bibliographical references and index.
Identifiers: LCCN 2019031527 | ISBN 978-0-593-12031-6 (trade pbk.) |
ISBN 978-0-593-12032-3 (lib. bdg.) | ISBN 978-0-593-12033-0 (ebook)
Subjects: LCSH: Mayflower (Ship)—Juvenile literature. | Massachusetts—
History—New Plymouth, 1620–1691—Juvenile literature. | Pilgrims
(New Plymouth Colony)—Juvenile literature.
Classification: LCC F68 .M53 2020 | DDC 974.4/02—dc23

Printed in the United States of America
10 9
First Edition

For Sarah, Marc, and Norah Galvin
at The Bookstore Plus

CONTENTS

You've probably heard about the *Mayflower*. Chances are, someone told you about the Pilgrims, who came to America because they wanted religious freedom. You probably learned how they crossed the wild Atlantic, how they landed at Plymouth Rock in Massachusetts, how the Wampanoag people taught them to grow corn, and how they all celebrated by sitting down together for a feast—the very first Thanksgiving. But only parts of that story are true.

There's a lot more to the history of the *Mayflower*, the Pilgrims, and the Wampanoag. So let's take a look at the historical documents, smash some of those old myths, and uncover the *real* story.

ONE

WHO WERE THE PILGRIMS, ANYWAY?

If April showers bring May flowers, what do May flowers bring?

The answer to the riddle, of course, is Pilgrims. The joke works because almost everyone knows a little about the Pilgrims. We've heard how they left England

and came to America in search of religious freedom. But that's not even close to the whole story. For starters, the Pilgrims didn't go to America when they left England. Not at first, anyway.

The real-deal story of the *Mayflower* begins way back in the 1530s, when King Henry VIII made some big changes to religion in England. King Henry wanted a son who could grow up to be the king of England, too. He and his first wife only had a daughter, though. Henry decided the solution was to get divorced and marry someone else, with whom he might have a son.

But the Roman Catholic Church was the official church in England then, and it did not allow divorce. King Henry went all the way to the pope, the leader of the whole Catholic Church, to argue that he should be able to leave his wife and marry a new one. When the pope said no, Henry decided to break away from the Catholic Church and start his own. From then on, the Church of England would be the official church of the land.

King Henry wasn't the only one who had issues with the Roman Catholic Church at that time. Many complained that Catholic leaders had too much power and wealth. But not everyone liked King Henry's new church, either. Some thought it was too similar to the Catholic Church. One group, called the Puritans, wanted the new church to be "purified" of all the old practices. Other people didn't think that was enough. They were called Separatists because they wanted to separate from the Church of England completely and have their own religion. The Separatists thought that true Christian believers should come together in their own small churches. They wanted those churches to be independent so members could study the Bible and make decisions on their own.

William Brewster, who was the postmaster of a village called Scrooby, decided to start a church in his own house. It was a risky idea. Back then, people who didn't follow the Church of England could be thrown in jail. In his book *Of Plymouth Plantation*, Pilgrim William Bradford wrote that Brewster's Separatists were "hunted and persecuted on every side."

Government officials were watching the Separatists' houses day and night. Some of them did get thrown in jail. You can probably understand why leaving England was starting to seem like a good idea.

So that's when the Separatists set sail for America, right?

Wrong. They went to Holland.

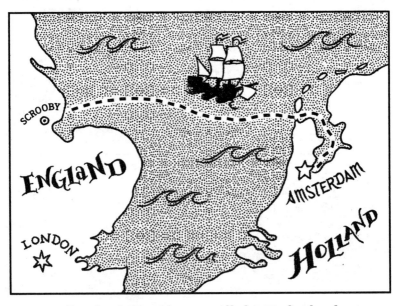

Holland, which today we call the Netherlands, was
known for religious freedom. Brewster learned that a
small group of Separatists had recently escaped to the
city of Amsterdam, where they could practice their
religion in peace. That seemed like a good idea, so
Brewster made plans to take his group there, too. His
followers were nervous, though. They didn't speak
Dutch. They weren't sure how they'd earn money to
support their families. Bradford later wrote that to
many of the Separatists, taking off for Holland seemed
like "an adventure almost desperate" and "a misery
worse than death." But after much discussion, they
decided to go anyway.

But Brewster didn't give up. About a year later, he took his group north in England and found another ship. Officials discovered their plan and tried to catch them again. But this time the Separatists saw the authorities coming. Most of the men had boarded the ship, and in a panic they brought up the anchor, hoisted the sails, and took off. The women and children, who hadn't boarded yet, were still waiting on the dock with most of their belongings.

English authorities caught the women and children. But then they weren't quite sure what to do with them, since their husbands and fathers were gone.

Eventually, the women and children were released and met up with the others in Holland. This group of Separatists lived in Amsterdam for about a year before deciding the busy port city wasn't the right place for them to settle. It was time to move on.

So that's when they left for Plymouth Rock, right?

Nope. Instead, they moved to another city in Holland, called Leiden.

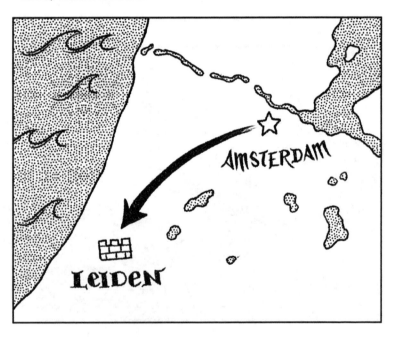

Leiden was a beautiful city with a university. It was also known for cloth making, and some of the newly arrived Separatists got jobs in that industry. They worked long hours at looms to weave linen and wool cloth. They would bring their products to the town chapel, where members of the local weavers' guild would examine them. If the cloth was judged to be of high-enough quality, then it could be sold.

Leiden was also home to a towering twelfth-century castle whose grounds had been turned into a public park. When Bradford and the other Separatists weren't working, they spent time there with their families.

Sounds pretty nice, doesn't it? But the Separatists weren't very happy in Leiden, either. The language sounded strange to them, and they weren't used to the Dutch customs.

Like Amsterdam, Leiden was a busy, bustling city. *Too* busy and bustling for many of the Separatists. They did their best to make a life there, but it never felt like home. Back in England, many of them had been farmers. They missed the countryside, and their farming skills didn't transfer well to such a big city. Some had trouble earning money. They were also worried that war might break out between Holland and Spain. And as the years passed, they grew more and more concerned that their English children were becoming Dutch. Some of the older kids had even run off to be soldiers or sailors.

The Separatists had wanted to break away from the Church of England, but they'd never meant to give up being English. There had to be a place where they could raise their families with the old English ways while practicing their religion in peace. So after about twelve years in Holland, they decided that the time had come to move again, to a place they could truly call home.

We're talking about Plymouth now, right? Actually, no. Not yet.

When the Separatists decided to leave Holland, they weren't sure at first where they'd go. For a while,

they were thinking about Guiana, on the northeast coast of South America. The Dutch had set up a colony there. It was lush and green, with warm weather that made it easy to grow food.

That sounds way better than the freezing-cold winters of New England, doesn't it? But the Separatists worried that the warm weather "would not agree so well with our English bodies." They feared that diseases would spread easily in the hot climate.

Another option was to cross the ocean but go farther north. There, they'd be living close to other English people. They worried about that, too. What if they were persecuted? What if it felt like England all over again? They'd have gone so far, all for nothing. What should they do?

It wasn't an easy decision. But in the end, William Brewster and his congregation made plans to say goodbye to Holland and set sail across the Atlantic.

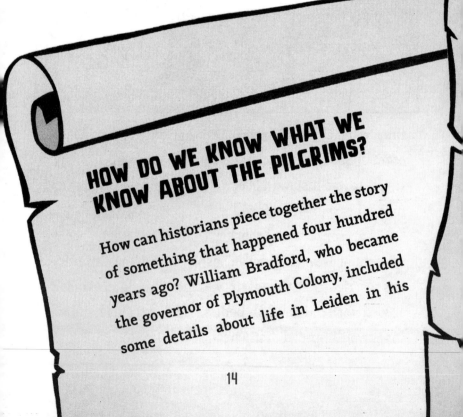

HOW DO WE KNOW WHAT WE KNOW ABOUT THE PILGRIMS?

How can historians piece together the story of something that happened four hundred years ago? William Bradford, who became the governor of Plymouth Colony, included some details about life in Leiden in his writings. And when the Pilgrims took off from Leiden in 1620, they left behind other clues, too.

Some of the buildings that were part of the Pilgrims' lives in Leiden are still there, including the old castle Burcht van Leiden and the chapel that also served as the guildhall, where the weavers had their cloth inspected.

BURCHT VAN LEIDEN

A fourteenth-century house that William Brewster supposedly visited while he was in Leiden is a museum now.

The Leiden American Pilgrim Museum displays artifacts from the years the Pilgrims

LEIDEN AMERICAN PILGRIM MUSEUM

spent in Leiden. Those everyday objects tell stories about daily life. Fragments of pipes and pottery dishes help historians piece together bits of the Separatists' days in Leiden. There's a lice comb from the 1500s—evidence that traveling packed together on ships and living in close quarters probably left the Pilgrims with itchy scalps. There are also toy soldiers and jacks. These suggest that play was an important part of the children's lives and that Pilgrim parents might not have been as stern and strict as we sometimes think.

As for the Pilgrims' lives in America, along with artifacts, we also have a couple of detailed primary sources to tell that story. A primary source is a firsthand account of something that happened, written by someone who was directly involved in it. Historians generally consider primary sources to be the most valuable references for understanding history.

Still, it's important to remember that historical writers had their own motivations and biases, just as people do today. And like modern people, seventeenth-century writers didn't know everything, so some of their writings include misunderstandings or assumptions that are just plain wrong. Really, a primary source isn't necessarily the truth of what happened; it's an account of what the writer noticed and believed at that time. And sometimes people lie in primary sources, too, sharing what they want others to believe instead of telling the whole truth.

One of the primary sources about the settlement of Plymouth, *Mourt's Relation*, is a collection of letters, documents, and journal entries mostly written by William Bradford and another Pilgrim settler, Edward Winslow, in 1620 and 1621.

The other main primary source about Plymouth is a book called *Of Plymouth Plantation*, which Bradford started writing in 1630. It's interesting to compare the two sources.

WAIT . . . WAS IT "PLYMOUTH" OR "PLIMOTH"?

In documents about this colony, you'll find its name spelled two different ways—"Plymouth" and "Plimoth." That's because back then, there was no standard spelling. William Bradford used the spelling "Plimoth" in his original history, so the living-history museum Plimoth Plantation chose to spell its name the same way. The modern city of Plymouth, Massachusetts, uses the other spelling.

Mourt's Relation was written close to the time the events were taking place, and parts of it are very detailed. That makes sense if you think about it. What do you remember more vividly—something that happened just last week, or something that happened five years ago? *Of Plymouth Plantation* was written almost a decade later, so it's what historians call a "recollection" of events, in which the writer does their best to remember what things were like.

Bradford's recollection still stands as one of

the few accounts of Plymouth written by someone who experienced it—and it was almost lost to us! For generations, Bradford's writings had been passed down among his descendants. Eventually, *Of Plymouth Plantation* ended up in the library of Boston's Old South Church.

The British occupied Boston during the Revolutionary War, and when the war ended, Bradford's manuscript was missing. It turned up years later in the library of the bishop of London and was printed there in 1856 and brought back to America in 1897.

OLD SOUTH CHURCH

DID PILGRIMS REALLY LOOK LIKE THAT?

Chances are, you've seen pictures of Pilgrims dressed all in black, with fancy buckles on their hats. Maybe when you were in preschool or kindergarten, you even made a hat like that out of construction paper and aluminum foil and wore it for your classroom's Thanksgiving celebration. But most of the time, Pilgrims didn't dress like that at all.

This is a situation where mythology—the stories told about a group of people—was accepted as history without proof. Often, modern people think of Pilgrims as being super strict and stern and dressing all in black. There *are* portraits of Pilgrims dressed in black, like the one of Edward Winslow on the next page. It's the only portrait of a Pilgrim painted from life, with the subject sitting there while the artist painted, and Winslow is indeed wearing black. But that's probably because people wore their best clothes to have their portraits made, and in the time of the Pilgrims, most people's best clothes were black.

Paintings like this one make it easy for people to assume that Pilgrims walked around in black clothes all the time. But historical documents tell a different story.

An estate inventory is a listing of a person's possessions. It includes all the things they owned at the time of their death. If that myth about Pilgrims wearing all black were true, you'd expect the estate listings from Plymouth Colony to be a long list of black pants and coats. But instead those documents list articles of clothing in all kinds of bright colors—red, yellow, orange, green, and violet, in addition to brown and black.

So when we look at historical documents, we see that the Pilgrims' world was probably a lot more colorful than many people thought.

TWO
VOYAGE ON THE *MAYFLOWER* (BUT NOT THE *SPEEDWELL*)

You might think this is the part of the story where the Pilgrims board the *Mayflower*, cross the ocean, land in Plymouth, and live happily ever after. But the real deal was more complicated than that.

For starters, the Pilgrims couldn't go anywhere until they figured out how to pay for the trip. It would be expensive. They didn't need just a ship. They needed enough supplies to last through the journey and their early days in the new colony. Brewster and his Separatists didn't have that kind of money. They needed to make a deal.

Let's Make a Deal!

THE SEPARATISTS MADE AN AGREEMENT WITH THE VIRGINIA COMPANY, WHICH HAD RECEIVED A CHARTER TO ESTABLISH SETTLEMENTS IN WHAT IS NOW CALLED NORTH AMERICA.

THE DEAL WORKED LIKE THIS: THE SEPARATISTS WOULD BE GIVEN SOME LAND, ALONG WITH MONEY AND SUPPLIES TO MAKE THE JOURNEY.

IN RETURN, ONCE THEY GOT SETTLED, THEY'D SEND NATURAL RESOURCES LIKE TIMBER, FURS, AND FISH BACK TO ENGLAND.

for England

The Virginia Company had already sent people to set up a colony in Jamestown and was making plans for another settlement, farther north. That's where the Pilgrims came into the picture.

The Virginia Company gave them a patent—a document giving them permission to settle in Virginia.

It's worth noting that their "permission" came from the king of England, who'd never set foot in Virginia. What made him think he had the right to give away land on a continent he'd never even visited?

The answer to that question has to do with a set of laws called the Doctrine of Discovery. It was based on a 1452 decree from the pope.

1452 decree

The Doctrine of Discovery said that Christian people could go into the lands of any non-Christians, take their land and resources, and enslave the people who lived there. People who weren't Christian weren't looked at as human beings.

By the 1620s, this was a popular belief, and it set the stage for Europeans to settle in other people's lands. So now the Pilgrims had a patent of their own, giving them permission from the king of England to settle in Virginia. But if you're imagining them sailing to the modern-day state of Virginia, you need to think again. In the time of the Pilgrims, the land that the English called the Colony of Virginia was way bigger than the state we know now. The colony actually stretched all the way from Jamestown north to the mouth of the Hudson River in what is now New York State. The patent that the Pilgrims received gave them permission to settle in the northern part of the Colony of Virginia, near the mouth of the Hudson River.

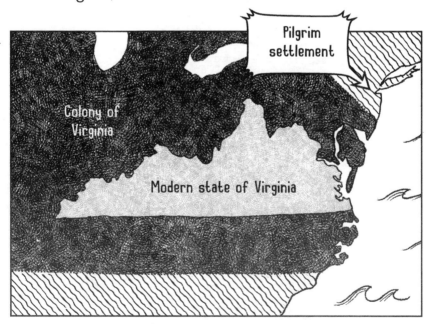

William Brewster's Separatists weren't the only ones who made the trip. Other people—known as adventurers—went, too. They weren't part of the Separatists' religious group. They wanted to go to America for other reasons. Some thought they might get rich in the new colonies, so they decided to tag along with the Separatists. It sounded like a perfect plan.

In July 1620, Brewster and the other Separatists in Leiden sold most of their possessions and boarded a ship. Can you guess the name of that ship?

If you guessed the *Mayflower*, guess again.

Their ship was called the *Speedwell*.

Brewster and his Separatists knew the journey would be long and dangerous, but they were ready. "The dangers were great, but not desperate; the difficulties were many, but not invincible," Bradford wrote.

It was finally time to set sail for Plymouth Rock.

Right?

Well . . . not yet. First, they set their course for the English port city of Southampton, where they would meet up with another ship. That ship had been hired by a different group of Separatists. They'd also decided to leave home and head for Virginia. They didn't have to sneak away, like Brewster's group; they'd been given permission to leave. They had hired a ship for their voyage, too. Can you guess the name of that one?

If you said the *Mayflower*, this time you're right! The ship was a hundred feet long and twenty-five feet wide, with three tall masts. The *Mayflower* and the *Speedwell* met in Southampton. With the two groups together, the Pilgrims' journey across the sea was ready to begin.

But before they even set out, there were signs that the trip wouldn't be all smooth sailing. The *Speedwell* had already sprung a leak and needed repairs. Once the work was complete, the two ships set sail. With good winds, they figured, they'd make it across the ocean in as little as six weeks.

That didn't work out. Almost immediately, the *Speedwell* started leaking again.

This time it was even worse. A passenger named Robert Cushman wrote about it in a letter to a friend.

If we had stayed at sea but three or four hours more, she would have sunk right down. And though she was twice trimmed at Hampton, yet now she is as open and leaky as a sieve.

You can't sail a sieve, so both ships turned around and went back to England. It took about a week for workers to fix the leaks.

When the repairs were complete, the Pilgrims set sail again. The next time they pulled into shore, they'd be in Plymouth.

But not Plymouth, Massachusetts.

Three hundred miles into the journey, the *Speedwell* started leaking yet again. So once more, both boats turned around. They ended up in the English city of Plymouth. And this time, the ship wasn't so easy to fix. They looked for the leak but couldn't find it. So what was the problem? Was the *Speedwell* just a crummy ship? Only one thing was certain: the *Speedwell* couldn't be fixed this time. The *Mayflower* would have to cross the ocean alone. So now what?

Some of the passengers decided that they didn't want to go to America after all. They should have been there by now! Instead, they'd spent six weeks at sea, only to end up back in England. Perhaps that was a sign that this new settlement wasn't such a great idea. (Mr. Cushman of the leaky-*Speedwell* letter was among those who called it quits.)

Summer had turned to September by the time the

rest of the passengers piled onto the *Mayflower*. They'd already used up a lot of their supplies, so they loaded more for the journey. Then the *Mayflower* left England with 102 passengers and about thirty crew members on board.

Finally they were on their way! But it would still be months before the Pilgrims made it to the place they would call Plymouth.

WHO CAME ON THE *MAYFLOWER*?

Some *Mayflower* passengers are well-known names in our history books, but others have interesting stories, too. Here are a few of the highlights.

FAMOUS *MAYFLOWER* PASSENGERS

These passengers are most often noted in histories written about Plymouth and the *Mayflower*. They are all men, which is no surprise, since the Pilgrims' society was patriarchal. That means it was controlled by men, and women weren't given equal rights or leadership roles.

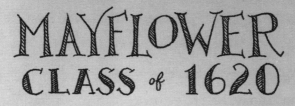

MAYFLOWER
CLASS of 1620

WILLIAM BRADFORD

WILLIAM BRADFORD would become Plymouth's most famous resident, but his trip didn't get off to a happy start. Not long after the *Mayflower* arrived in Provincetown Harbor, Bradford's wife Dorothy fell overboard and drowned. Bradford was elected governor of Plymouth after the colony's first governor, John Carver, died in April 1621. Bradford's book *Of Plymouth Plantation* is the most detailed history of the colony written by a *Mayflower* passenger.

WILLIAM BREWSTER was one of the Separatists who'd moved to Holland in 1608. While there, he continued to speak out about the Church of England and even ran a printing press that sent books and pamphlets full of his

WILLIAM BREWSTER

controversial ideas back to England. When the English found out, the authorities came after him, and he had to go into hiding for a couple of years. Brewster came to Plymouth on the *Mayflower* with his wife, Mary, and their two children named Love and Wrestling.

JOHN CARVER acted as governor of the *Mayflower* during the voyage. Then the settlers chose him as the colony's first governor.

JOHN CARVER

MYLES STANDISH was chosen to be the Pilgrims' military captain. He was involved in the early explorations of Cape Cod and helped to choose Plymouth as their permanent settlement. He's probably most famous for the poem that was written about him much later, though: "The Courtship of Miles Standish" by Henry Wadsworth Longfellow. The poem isn't historically accurate, but it made the Pilgrims featured in it pretty famous.

MYLES STANDISH

EDWARD WINSLOW

EDWARD WINSLOW was one of the early leaders of Plymouth, which was established in the territory of the Wampanoag people. Winslow led numerous expeditions to meet and trade with Native people in the area and wrote several firsthand accounts of his trips. These writings give us one perspective on the settlers' relations with the Wampanoag people.

JOHN ALDEN

JOHN ALDEN wasn't one of the Leiden Separatists; he worked as a cooper, or barrel maker, as part the *Mayflower*'s crew. But he ended up staying in Plymouth after he married Priscilla Mullins, who was orphaned when her family died during the first winter. He became an assistant governor of the colony. He's also known because he was featured in that Henry Wadsworth Longfellow poem, too.

NOT-SO-FAMOUS
MAYFLOWER PASSENGERS

These *Mayflower* passengers aren't as well known, but their stories are just as interesting!

THE DIDN'T-PACK-LIGHT AWARD

Mayflower passenger William Mullins was from an English town called Dorking. Among the luggage he brought to Plymouth were 250 shoes and thirteen pairs of boots. Spoiler: Mullins wasn't a seventeenth-century fashionista. He was a shoemaker.

THE FIRST-PILGRIM-MOTHER-TO-GIVE-BIRTH-AFTER-THE-VOYAGE AWARD

William and Susanna White came to Plymouth on the *Mayflower* with their five-year-old son, Resolved. Another son, Peregrine, was born on the ship in Provincetown Harbor soon after they arrived.

THE LAST-*MAYFLOWER*-SURVIVOR AWARD

Mary Allerton (Cushman) was four years old when she boarded the *Mayflower* with her parents, Isaac and Mary. She was the last surviving *Mayflower* passenger when she died, in 1699.

THE FAMILY-OF-TROUBLEMAKERS AWARD

John and Eleanor Billington came to Plymouth with their two sons, John and Francis. Not long after the *Mayflower* sailed into Plymouth Harbor, Francis shot off his father's musket near an open barrel of gunpowder and almost blew up the whole ship.

A few months later, his brother, John, got lost in the woods, where some Wampanoag men found him and took him to their village at Nauset, located in what is now called Eastham, on Cape Cod. The Plymouth settlers had to send a party out to go find him and get him back. The

Billington boys' dad was more than a trouble-maker. In 1630, he shot and killed another settler and ended up being sentenced to death by hanging.

THE ALMOST-DIDN'T-MAKE-IT AWARD

A servant named John Howland had an interesting voyage on the *Mayflower*. He was swept overboard during a storm and was almost lost at sea. Luckily, there was a rope trailing behind the ship. Howland managed to grab hold of it and pull himself up to the water's surface, where sailors spotted him and used a boat hook to pull him back onto the ship.

THE WE-WILL-SURVIVE AWARD

Elizabeth Tilley was about thirteen years old when she boarded the *Mayflower* with her parents, aunt, and uncle. She was the only one in her family who survived the first winter at Plymouth. Elizabeth ended up marrying John Howland, the guy who was almost lost at sea, and they had ten children. Their descendants include three presidents—Franklin Delano Roosevelt, George H. W. Bush, and George W. Bush.

THE ROWDY EDWARDS AWARD

Edward Doty and Edward Leister were both servants who came to Plymouth on the *Mayflower*. In June 1621, they got in a duel. Both Edwards got hurt in the fight and were punished afterward. Each was sentenced to have his head and feet tied together for a day, but the governor let both men off after just an hour.

THE "BEEN THERE, DONE THAT" AWARD

Sailing on the *Mayflower* wasn't Stephen Hopkins's first adventure. In 1609, he was on a voyage to Jamestown when a shipwreck in Bermuda stranded the passengers and crew on the island for ten months.

They survived on turtles, birds, and wild pigs and eventually built a ship and sailed the rest of the way to Jamestown. Hopkins went back to England but then decided to come to

Plymouth on the *Mayflower*. He brought his pregnant wife Elizabeth and their three kids, Constance, Giles, and Damaris. Little Oceanus Hopkins was born on the way—the only baby born on the *Mayflower* during its voyage.

WHO CAME *FROM* THE *MAYFLOWER?*

Only half of the *Mayflower*'s 102 passengers lived past the first winter in Plymouth, but many of those survivors started families. And then their families had families. And so on. Today, an estimated 35 million people are believed to be descendants of the *Mayflower*

Pilgrims. The Mayflower Society keeps a list of those who can prove their lineage, and it includes some pretty famous names.

Nine *Mayflower* descendants went on to become United States presidents.

John Adams

John Quincy Adams

Zachary Taylor

Ulysses S. Grant

James Garfield

Calvin Coolidge

Franklin Delano Roosevelt

George H. W. Bush

George W. Bush

Some were entertainers.

Actress
Marilyn Monroe

Singer
Bing Crosby

Actor
Christopher Reeve

I'M DREAMING OF A WHITE CHRISTMAS . . .

One was a famous chef.

Julia Child

One disguised herself as a man and fought in the Revolutionary War.

Deborah Sampson

One even walked on the moon.

Alan Shepard

44

And one became the first woman to fly a plane solo across the Atlantic. Imagine what the ladies who crossed the ocean on the *Mayflower* would think of that!

Amelia Earhart

THREE

JOURNEY ACROSS THE SEA

Once the Pilgrims left the leaky *Speedwell* behind, they were finally on their way, six weeks later than they'd planned. Some brought their families, but others wanted to see how things were in the new settlement first, so they left wives and children behind in Leiden, with plans to send for them later if everything worked out.

The Pilgrims used provisions lists from earlier settlement voyages to decide what to pack. The general rule was that you should arrive with everything you'd need for a year in the new settlement. The colonists packed bedding and warm clothes for New England's harsh winters. They knew they'd need muskets for defense and hunting. There would be no glass window-panes in the new settlement, so they packed oiled paper for their windows. They brought cotton yarn to use for wicks in their lamps, and kitchen supplies, too—cooking pots and kettles.

PEREGRINE WHITE CRADLE, PILGRIM HALL MUSEUM

When Susanna and William White boarded the *Mayflower*, they were expecting a baby, so they brought a cradle from Holland. Their son Peregrine was born just after they arrived.

Most of all, the Pilgrims needed food to survive the first winter. An autumn arrival meant that there wouldn't be time to plant and harvest crops before the cold weather arrived. What kind of foods could be packed to survive a six-week voyage across the ocean? Anything that wouldn't spoil—so no fresh meat, vegetables, or milk.

So what would you have eaten during the trip if you'd been on board the *Mayflower*?

A *MAYFLOWER* MENU

Biscuits

But these weren't the nice, soft, fluffy biscuits we eat with gravy today. They were hard and dry, so they wouldn't get moldy. And after a while, they became infested with little bugs called weevils. (But look on the bright side! At least that added some protein. . . .)

Dried peas and beans

Salted fish and beef tongues

Beer

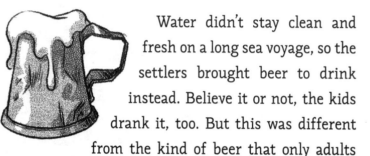

Water didn't stay clean and fresh on a long sea voyage, so the settlers brought beer to drink instead. Believe it or not, the kids drank it, too. But this was different from the kind of beer that only adults drink today. The Pilgrims called it "small beer," and it had less alcohol.

Lemons

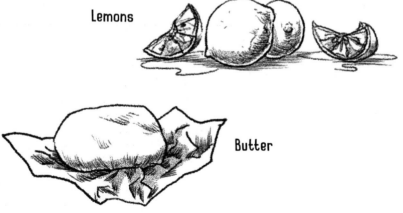

Butter

*absolutely NO substitutions

Later on, after the Pilgrims had arrived, settler Edward Winslow shared some advice when he wrote to a group that was about to make the trip: "Now because I expect your coming unto us with other of our friends, whose company we much desire, I thought good to advertise you of a few things needful." In other words: "Hey, we're really glad you're coming! Here's what you should bring."

Be careful to have a very good bread-room to put your biscuits in. Let your cask for beer and water be iron-bound for the first tier if not more.

Winslow likely offered this advice because he knew how difficult it was to keep food from spoiling during the voyage.

Trust not too much on us for corn at this time, for by reason of this last company that came, depending wholly upon us, we shall have little enough till harvest.

This was Winslow's nice way of saying "Please don't show up without food and expect to eat all of our corn, because we don't have that much."

> *Bring every man a musket or fowling-piece.*

In other words, make sure everybody brings a gun. By the time Winslow wrote this, he knew there were plenty of ducks and geese in Plymouth.

> *Bring juice of lemons, and take it fasting; it is of good use.*

Lemons prevented scurvy—a disease caused by a lack of vitamin C. Sailors and other travelers often got scurvy during long sea voyages when there was no access to fresh fruits or vegetables. If you got scurvy, your muscles would ache, your gums would bleed, and your teeth would start falling out, so it was worth it to plan ahead and bring those lemons.

> *If you bring anything for comfort in the country, butter or salad oil, or both is very good.*

Winslow probably included butter because there was no way to make it in Plymouth. The Pilgrims brought pigs, goats, and chickens on the *Mayflower*, but no cows.

If you're thinking that all those supplies didn't leave much room for people, you're right. The *Mayflower* wasn't very big to begin with. We don't have the original plans, so no one can be sure exactly what the ship looked like. But based on documents we do have, historians believe the *Mayflower*'s living space was about eighty feet long and twenty-four feet wide.

Imagine a high school basketball court cut in half the long way. Now imagine living in that space for a little over two months with 101 people—some friends and some strangers—all of your stuff, and also some cats, dogs, pigs, chickens, and goats. Welcome to the *Mayflower*.

The sixty-six-day trip across the ocean couldn't have been comfortable. For starters, the *Mayflower* was built to carry cargo, not passengers. The ship had transported wine and cloth before being hired to haul the Pilgrims across the Atlantic. Given what historians know about the design of most cargo ships, they believe the Pilgrims probably stored their goods on the lowest levels of the *Mayflower*. Passengers lived in the area just above that, known as the tween deck. That space would have been cold, dark, stuffy, damp, and only about five feet high.

WHAT DID THE MAYFLOWER LOOK LIKE?

There are many paintings and models of the *Mayflower*, but nobody knows how accurate they are. Historians never found the original plans or drawings for the ship, so all we know is its approximate size and what kind of ship it was. Based on that, historians, model builders, and artists had to guess what it must have looked like.

In the middle of the twentieth century, those educated guesses were used to create a replica, or copy, of the *Mayflower*, called the *Mayflower II*. The new ship is about the same size as the original but has four masts. When it was completed in England in 1957, it sailed to America using the same route as the Pilgrims. Then the *Mayflower II* docked in Plymouth, where it became part of Plimoth Plantation, a living-history museum about the colony.

But what happened to the original *Mayflower*? You'd think that the famous ship that

brought the Pilgrims to America would be pre-
served for everyone to see, but the truth is, the
Mayflower just sort of faded away. The ship left
Plymouth to go back to England on April 5,
1621. Even though it had been a miserable winter, none of the original Pilgrims returned with
the ship. After making it across the Atlantic,
the *Mayflower* went back to hauling cargo, but
within a few years, the ship was worn out and
in pretty rough shape. The last record of the
Mayflower is an assessment of its value in 1624,
when the ship was described as being "in ruins"
and valued at about 128 English pounds.

The Pilgrims were absolutely packed onto the ship when it set sail that September. They knew they were facing a long list of dangers—storms, pirates, illness, maybe falling overboard—but at least they were finally going somewhere.

"These troubles being blown over, and now all being compact together in one ship, they put to sea again with a prosperous wind," William Bradford wrote of their departure.

And then they got seasick.

The voyage across the Atlantic was rough and stormy, so it wasn't long before the passengers were feeling queasy. You'd think the sailors would help them out, but Bradford wrote about one crew member who did just the opposite. He kept making fun of people who got seasick. Bradford called that guy "a proud and very profane young man" who actually told the seasick passengers that "he hoped to help cast half of them overboard before they came to their journey's end." That's what happened to people who died in the middle of a voyage—their bodies were thrown over the side of the ship.

A little while later, Bradford seemed pretty happy

to report that the bullying sailor was actually the one who died.

"*But it pleased God before they came half seas over, to smite this young man with a grievous disease, of which he died in a desperate manner, and so was himself the first that was thrown overboard.*"

The seasickness continued, and the storms took a toll on the ship as well as her passengers. Sometimes the winds were so strong that the ship literally got blown backward. (That's why the ocean crossing took so long. The *Mayflower's* average speed was about two miles per hour. The passengers could have walked faster than that!) The ship got leakier and leakier. When it was almost halfway across the ocean, a huge wave hit and cracked one of its timbers. Bradford wrote that the sailors used "a great iron screw the passengers brought out of Holland" to raise the beam back into place.

That sixty-six-day voyage must have felt like it was lasting forever, but William Bradford didn't spend much time writing about the voyage itself. He skipped ahead to when they spotted land at daybreak on November 9, 1620, "and they were not a little joyful."

The only question was . . . where were they?

MOVE OVER, *MAYFLOWER*

The *Mayflower* is certainly the most famous ship that set sail for Plymouth, but it's not the only one.

THE *FORTUNE*

The *Fortune* made it to Plymouth in 1621 with thirty-five passengers on board. Bradford and the others who'd arrived the year before were thrilled to see more English settlers, but it sure would have been nice if they'd brought enough food and supplies to take care of themselves. "The plantation was glad of this addition of strength," Bradford wrote, "but could have wished that many of them had been of better condition, and all of them better furnished with provisions. But that could not now be helped."

THE *PARAGON*

More settlers were hoping to sail to Plymouth on the *Paragon* in 1622, but it was leaking before it even left England, and then a storm did more damage. Once the *Paragon* was fixed, the crew set sail. But there were more storms in the North Atlantic. One of them wiped out the ship's whole upper works, and the *Paragon* had to go back to England. It never made it to Plymouth.

THE *ANNE* AND THE *LITTLE JAMES*

Both the *Anne* and the *Little James* arrived in Plymouth in 1623, carrying about ninety passengers. They included some of the wives and children of the earlier settlers, who had stayed behind in Leiden.

THE *CHARITY*

The *Charity* arrived in Plymouth in 1624 with more settlers and goods. Among its passengers were the first cattle to arrive in the new colony. The Pilgrims were pretty excited about that because until then they'd had only goats' milk.

WHEN IS A PILGRIM NOT A PILGRIM?

If you'd been alive in 1620 and you asked about the Pilgrims, there's a good chance no one would have understood who you were talking about. That's because the Pilgrims weren't called Pilgrims back then. Primary sources from the time refer to all the passengers from the first ships that sailed to New England as "First Comers." That includes people who came on the *Mayflower* in 1620—some were Separatists and some weren't—as well as the settlers who arrived on the *Fortune* a year later; the *Anne* and the *Little James*, which landed in 1623; and the *Charity*, which showed up in 1624.

The word "Pilgrims" wasn't used to describe the earliest Plymouth settlers during their lifetimes. William Bradford did use the word once in his book about Plymouth, when he described the Separatists leaving Holland: "They knew they were pilgrims, and looked not much on those things, but lift up their eyes to the heavens, their dearest country, and quieted their spirits." In those days, the word "pilgrim" (with a lowercase *p*) referred to anyone who made a journey for religious reasons. It wasn't until the 1800s that people started using "Pilgrim" with a capital *P* to refer to the Plymouth settlers.

FOUR
WELCOME TO PLYMOUTH ROCK! (OR MAYBE NOT . . .)

The Pilgrims were overjoyed to spot land after more than two months at sea.

Finally! The moment we've been waiting for . . . when the Pilgrims take that first step onto Plymouth Rock. Right?

Wrong.

Because that land the Pilgrims spotted wasn't Plymouth.

It also wasn't Virginia. It was the place we today call Cape Cod, in Massachusetts. So now what?

Cape Cod seemed like a fine place. There was a bay with plenty of fish to catch. The Pilgrims didn't care

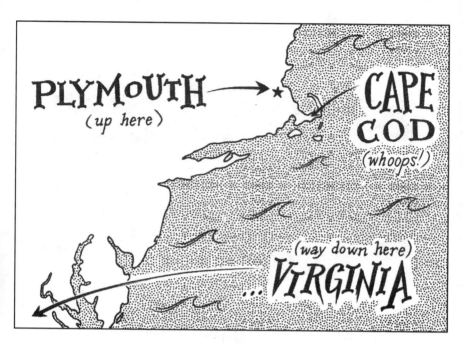

that the Native people who already lived there had their own laws and rules for how others should enter their territory. But the Pilgrims did care that the king of England hadn't given them permission to settle in that exact place. Their patent was for an area of land more than two hundred miles away. They had to at least try to make it to the Hudson.

It was a risky decision. The crew didn't have charts for this part of the coast, and the captain knew they might run aground. For a while it was smooth sailing, but when the tide changed, the *Mayflower* found itself in the middle of a bunch of dangerous shoals. It was a treacherous area for ships. The explorer Samuel de Champlain had run aground there in 1606. Would the *Mayflower* suffer the same fate?

Luckily for the Pilgrims, the wind changed, and when the tide came in, they were able to get away from all those shoals. Cape Cod was looking pretty great by then, so they decided to turn back and worry about the patent later. On November 11, 1620, the *Mayflower* anchored in Cape Cod Bay.

The Pilgrims realized they were on shaky legal ground because they'd landed in a place where they had no permission to settle. Also, they were three thousand miles from England, and nobody was really in charge of anything. There was no official body here to make laws, and there were no judges to settle disputes. The Pilgrims decided they needed some kind of agreement—a simple promise that they'd work together and be bound by laws that they would set for themselves. That document was the Mayflower Compact, and every man would be required to sign it before he left the ship.

THE MAYFLOWER COMPACT

The night before the *Mayflower* passengers went ashore in Cape Cod, they decided they needed an agreement to keep everyone working together. But by then, it was a challenge to agree on much of anything.

They were a mix of Separatists and adventurers, religious people and not-so-religious people. They didn't have a whole lot in common, and they were already facing hardships. Many were weak and sick from the trip. Winter was upon them. And here they were, in a place where they technically didn't even have permission to settle.

There were already whispers of trouble. Some men were talking about going off on their own. Others were certain that the only way any of them could survive the winter was by working together. They decided that a formal agreement was the only way to ensure their survival. So that night, before they left the ship, they

wrote the Mayflower Compact and chose John Carver to be their governor for the first year.

You might have heard about the Mayflower Compact—that it was an early version of the United States Constitution. But that's not really the best explanation. The Constitution is an outline for the U.S. government—a document that sets up how the whole thing works. The Constitution lays out the branches of government: the president and vice president, the Senate and the House of Representatives, and the U.S. Supreme Court. The Constitution details the responsibilities and powers of each branch, and the limits on those powers, as well as the rights of citizens. The Mayflower Compact was a lot simpler than that. In fact, the whole thing is pretty short:

"Having undertaken, for the glory of God and advancement of the Christian faith and honor of our King and country, a voyage to plant the first colony in the northern parts of Virginia, do these present solemnly and mutually in the presence of God and one of another, covenant and combine ourselves together into a civil body politic, for our better ordering and preservation, and furtherance of the ends aforesaid; and by virtue hereof to enact, constitute, and frame such just and equal laws, ordinances, acts, constitutions, and offices, from time to time, as shall be thought most meet and convenient for the general good of the colony, unto which we promise all due submission and obedience."

Translation: We came here to establish a colony, and now we agree to work together and create a government to keep things under control. We'll come up with some laws that will help the colony, and we promise to follow those.

The Mayflower Compact wasn't really a list of laws so much as it was an agreement to make some and follow them later on. It also wasn't the first example of a democratic government in the new colonies. The year before, Virginia had set up the House of Burgesses, which created a representative government for men who owned land. And Wampanoag people were practicing democracy long, long before that. Their sachems, or leaders of the communities, followed ancient systems where everyone in the community had the ability to share their voices in decisions that would affect them.

But the Mayflower Compact was significant for a few reasons. For starters, it was put together by people who were three thousand miles from home, with no one officially in charge. It established the idea that people should agree on laws together. It also laid a foundation for the separation of church and state—the idea that the government shouldn't be run by religious leaders and shouldn't tell anyone how to worship. You might be surprised that people as religious as the Separatists were on board with setting things up that way. After all, they had left their country to follow their religion. But the Separatists understood that they made up only about half of the Plymouth community and that the new settlement depended on the others, too. They'd also just come from a place where people didn't get to make their own decisions about religion, and that hadn't worked out well for them.

Every man who was healthy enough had to sign the Mayflower Compact. He could either sign his name or, if he couldn't write, mark an X. Forty-one men ended up signing. The other nine likely were too sick to sign or were sailors who'd only been hired for a year and didn't plan to stay. No women signed the Mayflower Compact. Unfortunately, the idea that women shouldn't have a say in government also arrived with the Pilgrims on the *Mayflower*, and that practice persisted in America for many years to come.

Once the Mayflower Compact had been signed, the Pilgrims were ready to explore. They couldn't move off the *Mayflower* yet, because they didn't have anywhere else to live. They weren't even sure they were going to stay in Cape Cod. But they wanted to send some men ashore to check the place out. They'd brought along a shallop—a smaller boat that could be used for exploring the coastline and rivers—but it had been broken into several pieces for the journey, so the carpenters had to put it back together before they could use it. In the meantime they used a smaller boat to send some men to shore to get wood.

Right away the Pilgrims noticed that Cape Cod had a lot to offer. There were ducks and geese and even whales!

They wished they'd brought along the right equipment to hunt the whales so they could have harvested the oil. The men caught some small fish near the shore and found shellfish, too. They were excited about the great supply of fat mussels—until everybody who ate them got sick.

"They caused us to cast and scour, but they were soon all well again." —EDWARD WINSLOW

Translation: They threw up and had diarrhea but felt better after a while.

Another problem was the weather. The Pilgrims had arrived later than planned, and Cape Cod was cold in November. The bay was too shallow for them to bring the boats to shore, so anyone who wanted to get to land had to wade through the cold water.

On November 13, some of the men brought the shallop on land to work on it, and other passengers came onshore to get cleaned up. (Two months is a long time to be on a ship without a bath!) A couple of days later, sixteen men went out exploring, led by Captain Myles Standish. After they'd gone about a mile, they saw five or six people and a dog. These were Wampanoag people, and when they saw Standish and the other men, they ran into the woods and whistled for their dog to come, too. The Pilgrim men went after them, following their tracks for miles that night, but never caught up.

The next day the Pilgrim men picked up the tracks again. They led to a valley with deer and freshwater springs. Imagine how great it must have tasted to them after months of drinking warm, weak beer on a ship!

As the Pilgrim men kept exploring, they saw more signs of Wampanoag people who had lived in the area. Winslow wrote that they had come upon plenty of land that looked good for farming. He could tell that Native people had been using it to plant corn.

The Pilgrim men also found a little path that led to some piles of sand covered with old mats. They started digging there and found a bow and arrows. Soon the men realized that they were disturbing a grave and decided they should leave it alone.

"Because we thought it would be odious unto them to ransack their sepulchres." —EDWARD WINSLOW

Translation: Only really rotten people would go digging around in other people's graves.

But a little later that day, the Pilgrim men dug up some corn that the Wampanoag people had placed in a storage pit. The Pilgrims decided it would be okay to steal that. They took as much as they could carry, buried the rest and planned to return for it later, and started back to their ship. Winslow wrote that they talked about paying for it somehow later on.

The next day, they got lost in the woods and found a deer trap made out of a sapling. What followed was a scene that would have made the Pilgrims' Funniest Home Videos list, if only the Pilgrims had cameras.

"As we wandered we came to a tree, where a young sprit {sapling} was bowed down over a bow, and some acorns strewed underneath. Stephen Hopkins said it had been to catch some deer. So as we were looking at it, William Bradford being in the rear, when he came looked also upon it, and as he went above, it gave a sudden jerk up, and he was immediately caught by the leg." —EDWARD WINSLOW

After the other men got Bradford untangled, they headed for shore and found their ship again.

As November marched on, the Pilgrims sent more exploring parties to shore. *Mayflower* captain Christopher Jones led a group of thirty-four men on an expedition through terrible weather that Winslow thought probably led to some of the men's deaths later.

But Jones pressed on with his group of men. They found the rest of the stored corn and stole what they'd left behind the first time. Then they found another storage pit and stole that corn, too, planning to use it for seed. Winslow wrote that finding the corn was "God's good providence," and this time there was no mention of paying anyone back for it. They also found another grave. They seemed less concerned about disturbing this one. They dug it up, took some of what Winslow called "the prettiest things," and buried the body again.

The men also found some empty homes, and Winslow's writing provides some of the first English descriptions of the homes that Wampanoag people in this region built.

"*The houses were made with long young sapling trees,
bended and both ends stuck into the ground. They were
made round, like unto an arbor, and covered down to the
ground with thick and well wrought mats; and the door was
not over a yard high, made of a mat to open. The chimney
was a wide open hole in the top, for which they had a
mat to cover it close when they pleased.*"

Inside the homes, the Pilgrim men found deer heads and baskets full of acorns and pieces of fish. There were also bundles of cattail and bulrush reeds for making mats. Again, the men helped themselves to what they wanted. Winslow said they'd meant to leave behind some beads as a sign of peace before they went back to their shallop. But they got busy with other things and forgot. "But as soon as we can meet conveniently with them, we will give them full satisfaction," Winslow wrote.

At that point the Pilgrims had a decision to make. Some thought they should just stay where they were and settle in Cape Cod. After all, it had a pretty nice harbor, even though it was shallow for the big ship. Fishing would probably be good, and they kept seeing whales. Also, the weather was wintry; it wasn't a good time to move.

WHALING WHOOPS!

In *Mourt's Relation*, Edward Winslow wrote about the Pilgrims' failed attempt to hunt one of the whales they spotted. A man tried to shoot a whale that came close to the ship, but his musket exploded. Nobody got hurt, including the whale, which swam away.

But others wanted to explore further. They thought there might be a place with more reliable sources of fresh water and a better harbor for ships and fishing. What if they settled in Cape Cod only to find that they'd chosen the wrong place? They'd have to uproot themselves and start all over again. They wanted to be sure. So the Pilgrims sent some men to explore a harbor to the north.

DECEMBER 1620

"THE WATER FROZE ON OUR CLOTHES AND MADE THEM MANY TIMES LIKE COATS OF IRON."

THE NEXT DAY, WHEN THE MEN ARRIVED AT ANOTHER BAY, THEY SAW ABOUT A DOZEN WAMPANOAG PEOPLE ONSHORE, CUTTING UP A BIG FISH.

THE SEPARATISTS DIDN'T TALK WITH THEM, BUT LATER THEY FOUND MORE HOMES AND GRAVES.

AND THAT NIGHT . . .

NOTE: THE PILGRIMS USED THE GENERAL TERM "INDIANS" TO DESCRIBE NATIVE PEOPLE THEY MET IN NEW ENGLAND. TODAY WE KNOW THAT THESE WERE WAMPANOAG PEOPLE, WHO HAD BEEN LIVING IN THE REGION FOR THOUSANDS OF YEARS. THESE PARTICULAR MEN WERE PROBABLY THE SAME PEOPLE WHOSE CORN THE SEPARATISTS HAD STOLEN.

The Pilgrims called the spot where this happened "the First Encounter," and the name stuck. Today that place is still called First Encounter Beach, on Eastham, in Cape Cod.

Meanwhile the Pilgrims set out in their shallop, still looking for a better harbor. Another storm kicked up, and the hinges broke on their rudder, so they couldn't use it to steer anymore. They ended up in a harbor none of them had ever seen before. And it looked like a fine place to live.

"On Monday they sounded the harbor and found it fit for shipping," William Bradford wrote. He observed the cornfields that had been prepared by the Wampanoag people and the brooks for fresh water. It seemed like a fine place to settle, so the exploring team went back to the ship to share the news. Finally, the *Mayflower* passengers would have a place to call home. And, yes, this time it was the place they'd call Plymouth. But you might have noticed that nobody mentioned that rock.

SMASHING THE STORY
OF PLYMOUTH ROCK

If you visit Plymouth, Massachusetts, today, you might see crowds of people streaming off tour buses to stare at a rock on the city's waterfront. That's Plymouth Rock. Tour guides will tell you it's the legendary landing spot of the Pilgrims. The key word here is "legendary."

Because no one knows if a single Pilgrim ever set foot on that famous rock.

There's absolutely no mention of the rock in any of the primary sources from the seventeenth century. None. Edward Winslow didn't talk about it in *Mourt's Relation*, nor did William Bradford mention it in *Of Plymouth Plantation*. Nobody ever talked about the rock until 1741.

That year, the town of Plymouth was planning to build a wharf on the waterfront, over an old rock that had always been there.

And that's when Thomas Faunce spoke up. He was ninety-four or ninety-five years old, the son of a Plymouth settler who'd arrived in 1623. He said people had told him that the rock was the landing spot of the original *Mayflower* Pilgrims. That was the first anyone else had ever heard of it.

Plymouth Rock got a lot

more famous in 1774, on the eve of the Revolutionary War, when a group of Plymouth citizens chose the rock as a symbol for the Patriot cause. They decided that sharing the story of the Pilgrims—those brave people who had broken away from England—would be a perfect way to get people fired up against Great Britain. They made a plan to move Plymouth Rock from the waterfront to the town square. They'd put it next to the liberty pole so people would rally around it and join their cause. It was a brilliant idea . . .

Until they broke the rock. In the process of loading Plymouth Rock into a carriage, they split it right in half.

Undaunted, they left the bottom half at the waterfront and took the top half to the town square. They made the best of the fact that they'd busted their symbol of liberty by telling people that the broken rock was a sign that the American colonies needed to split from Great Britain.

No one knows how much the rock helped their cause, but the Continental Army did win the Revolutionary War, and the colonies broke free from Great Britain. The Sons of Liberty didn't need Plymouth Rock at the town hall anymore, and in 1834, it was moved to the lawn of Pilgrim Hall Museum.

Meanwhile, people had been using hammers and chisels to chip pieces off the half left

on the waterfront. One of those chunks was eventually donated to the Smithsonian's National Museum of American History. It was from Lewis Bradford, a descendant of William Bradford, who confessed to his vandalism with the words he painted on the rock.

Broken from the MOTHER ROCK by Mr Lewis BRADFORD, on TUESDAY 28th of Decr 1830. 4½ o'clock PM. MR. { SCADDING. } Whilne? the PILGRIMS MR. { SHAW. } Landed upon thi ROCK Decr 11th 1720. o.s.

In 1880, the two halves of Plymouth Rock were reunited when the Pilgrim Hall piece was brought back to the waterfront. Someone carved the date 1620 on the rock, and the display was redesigned. Today the rock lives in a little cage just off Water Street. It's about a third of its original size, and much of it is buried in sand. People still come to take pictures, even though there's no historical evidence to prove it's anything other than a glued-together slab of granite.

WHAT'S WRONG WITH THIS PICTURE?

The story of Pilgrims stepping onto Plymouth Rock may just be a myth, but that hasn't stopped artists from showing it over and over in their paintings of the historic landing. Here's one of the famous paintings that hangs at Pilgrim Hall Museum in Plymouth. Take a close look and see if you think it's historically accurate.

The Landing of the Pilgrims by Michel Felice Corné (1803–1806)

Not surprisingly, this painting makes a big deal of showing the Pilgrims landing on that rock, but there's another detail that's not quite in line with historical documents. In Winslow's and Bradford's writings, there's no mention at all of Wampanoag men waiting onshore when the Pilgrims landed. In fact, both men note just the opposite—the absence of people. This might be because the artist cared more about making a cool painting than about historical accuracy.

Interestingly, we don't tend to see the same mistake in paintings created later in the 1800s. These pieces from the second half of the century include the legendary rock but leave out the Native people.

Landing of the Pilgrims on Plymouth Rock, 1620 by Peter Rothermel (1869 engraving based on an 1854 painting)

Landing of the Pilgrims by Henry A. Bacon (1877)

This probably has less to do with the artists' attention to historical accuracy and more to do with American beliefs at the time. By the middle of the 1800s, an idea called manifest destiny had taken hold—the belief that English settlers were meant to spread across North America and reshape the land, regardless of what happened to Native peoples as a result.

Reminders that Native people were here first didn't really support the notion of manifest destiny. As a result, Native people tend to be either missing or misrepresented as wild and savage in art created during this time period.

FIVE

PEOPLE OF THE FIRST LIGHT

The Pilgrims often wrote about their new home as a wild, unsettled place. William Bradford called it "a hideous and desolate wilderness." But of course, the land that became Plymouth was not really empty or desolate. And this wasn't a secret. Turn the page and take a look at the map Samuel de Champlain created when he explored the area in 1605.

Champlain described it as having "a great many cabins and gardens," and he wrote of meeting Native people out fishing in canoes. They even gave Champlain some of their hooks.

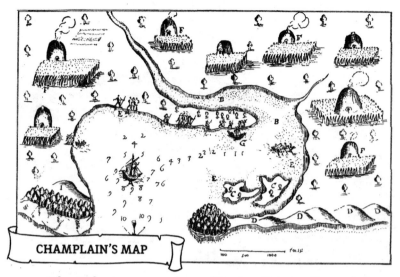

CHAMPLAIN'S MAP

The Pilgrims may have liked talking about their desolate wilderness, but that's not the real deal at all. The truth is, the Wampanoag people had lived there for more than twelve thousand years. They'd built homes there, raised their families, and farmed the land long before the Pilgrims ever showed up.

Who were the Wampanoag people? One thing that's clear from seventeenth-century documents is that the English settlers didn't understand the answer to that question. They wrote about the Native people they met, providing us with some primary documents about the Wampanoag people. But those documents are limited by the Pilgrims' perspective. The Pilgrims didn't speak the Wampanoag language or understand

Wampanoag culture. Also, it's important to remember that the English were aiming to colonize, or take over, the land. That was more difficult to justify if you had to admit you were stealing it from people who had lived there successfully for thousands of years. So in some of their documents, the English had an interest in describing the Wampanoag people as less advanced than they really were.

One letter in that famous primary source *Mourt's Relation* is called "Reasons and Considerations Touching the Lawfulness of Removing out of England into the Parts of America." In other words, "Here are some thoughts on whether it's okay for us to move out of England and settle on this land in America."

In this letter, the writer, Robert Cushman, asked, "But some will say, what right have I to go live in the heathens' country?" When he wrote "heathens," he was, of course, referring to Wampanoag people, who practiced their own religion, rather than the religion of the Pilgrims. He went on to suggest that the English had every right to settle in America because they were praying for the Wampanoag people to be converted to Christianity.

Cushman's ideas were based on the Doctrine of Discovery, which said it was fine for Christians to steal the lands of non-Christian people and enslave them. Cushman believed that God wanted the Pilgrims to convert the Native people, and that could only happen if they lived in the same place. The Native people couldn't go to England, because England was full. So the Pilgrims had to move to America so they could start converting people to their religion. Done.

At this point, you might be thinking,

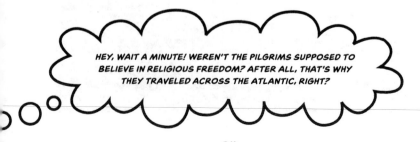

HEY, WAIT A MINUTE! WEREN'T THE PILGRIMS SUPPOSED TO BELIEVE IN RELIGIOUS FREEDOM? AFTER ALL, THAT'S WHY THEY TRAVELED ACROSS THE ATLANTIC, RIGHT?

Well . . . yes and no. The Pilgrims wanted freedom to practice their religion without being persecuted. But at the same time, they believed that it was their job to convert other people to their religion. Even if those people had a religion they liked just fine. So the Pilgrims and colonists who came later used the idea of converting Native people to help justify moving onto their land.

The rest of Cushman's letter goes on to describe how Native people were using the land—or not using it. He got that completely wrong—but claimed that it was proof that the English were right to take the land.

Cushman called the land "spacious and void." He wrote that the Native people who lived there were "not industrious, neither have art, science, skill, or faculty to use either the land or the commodities of it, but all spoils, rots, and is marred for want of manuring, gathering, ordering, etc." In other words, he said the people weren't hardworking and weren't using the land, so it was just going to waste. Therefore, it was fine for the English to take the land and use it.

Cushman's arguments were way off base. This is an example of a primary source that shows what someone was thinking at the time—but the information it gives us is incorrect. We can't time-travel and interview Cushman to find out whether he was really that ignorant about Wampanoag culture or whether he was misrepresenting Wampanoag people on purpose to make an excuse for stealing their land (or maybe a little of both?). Either way, Cushman got it wrong.

Archaeology—the study of objects from a culture—and Wampanoag oral history provide us with a better answer to the question "Who were the Wampanoag people?" And what do we know about them from what they left behind?

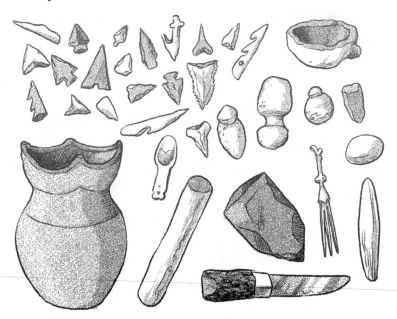

The tools, pottery, jewelry, fishhooks, arrow and spear points, and other items unearthed from their villages tell us that the Wampanoag people were makers. They built the frames for their homes—dome-shaped buildings called wetuash (WEE-too-ash)—out of cedar saplings and covered them with layers of cattail reed mats. In the winter they'd move inland, into bigger longhouses, where multiple families lived together. There they'd cook over fires. It was too hot for that in the summer months, so families used outdoor kitchens then.

An outdoor Wampanoag kitchen at Plimoth Plantation

If you visited a Wampanoag kitchen, you might find anything from fish and shellfish to corn, beans, and squash, to a porridge called nausamp, made of ground corn with fruit and nuts and cooked in a clay pot.

The Wampanoag people made dugout canoes called mishoonash from hollowed-out trees. They'd burn and scrape the inside of the log to shape the boat. They made fish nets out of basswood fiber and clothing out

A Wampanoag mishoon at Plimoth Plantation

of deer skins. They made clay pots that could be used for cooking over a fire. They made knives out of a rock called basalt and used them for butchering meat and preparing hides to make clothing. They also used stone to make tools, including axes, drills, and gouges.

Can you imagine someone using the phrase "not industrious" to describe the people who did all that?

The Wampanoag people were also ecologists—people who understood the relationships between the plants, animals, earth, and themselves. And they were indeed making use of the land. The area surrounding Cape Cod and Plymouth was full of the things Wampanoag people needed to sustain their lives.

The Wampanoag people gathered reeds for mats and baskets. They managed the woodlands through controlled burns—small-scale fires that created a better habitat for wildlife. Wampanoag women used hoes made of clamshells and bone to till the land. They planted corn with beans and squash. Seeing women at work planting struck the English settlers as strange; in their culture, farming was a job for men. When the Wampanoag people grew crops such as corn, beans, and squash, they took care to rotate where they planted

so that the soil wouldn't be depleted. Wampanoag people believed that when they took something, they had a responsibility to give back through prayer, thanksgiving, and ceremonies.

Wampanoag men were also hunters and fishermen. They hunted deer, beavers, foxes, otters, martens, wildcats, rabbits, seals, fowl, and small mammals. In the winter they hunted larger game animals, like deer. They ate the meat, made bedding and clothing from the hides, and used the tendons for sewing and making tools. Wampanoag people made spears, bows, and arrows. They crafted fishhooks and various kinds of nets, too, and used these in both the ocean and rivers. They caught fish, whales, shellfish, and eels. So much for not being industrious!

Wampanoag people had the knowledge and ability to make everything they needed for their lives. They gathered all materials for their houses, clothing, furnishings, tools, weapons, boats, and jewelry of all kinds. Archaeologists have uncovered pieces of jewelry made from bone, stone, copper, brass, and different kinds of shell. Wampanoag people used these materials to make earrings, necklaces, bracelets, and hair pieces. They also made string and cord from a variety of plant fibers and then wove sashes, legging ties, and many types of bags and baskets.

Community has always been important to the Wampanoag people. In the days of the Pilgrims, the Wampanoag people were citizens who had their own form of government.

Their sachems were chosen for their character and integrity. They held councils to talk about issues and decisions and to care for people in their community. The Wampanoag people formed confederations with other nations so that they could talk about common concerns.

Wampanoag people traded with other nations, too. There's been a lot written about the English trading beads and furs with Native people, but the truth is that Native people had set up far-reaching trade routes across the continent before Europeans arrived. Geological clues tell us a little about how far those routes might have stretched. When archaeologists were excavating a Plymouth-area site in 2016, they found a flake of Ramah chert, a rock that's good for toolmaking. It's a rare material that's found only in Labrador, Canada, so what was it doing in New England?

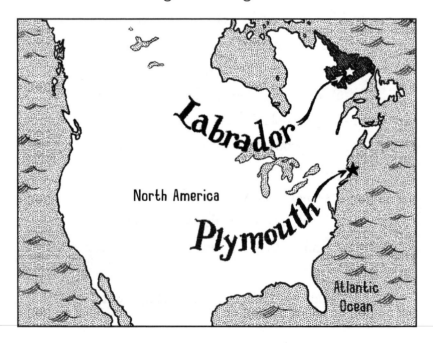

For archaeologists, it's a clue that the Wampanoag people had connections with other Native communities more than a thousand miles away.

Some of this rich culture was lost for a long time because of colonization, but through the years, Wampanoag people have worked to keep their traditions alive. Zerviah Gould Mitchell was a descendant of Massasoit, who was a Wampanoag sachem when the Pilgrims arrived.

During her lifetime in the 1800s, Mitchell wove baskets and taught her daughters that tradition. She published a book about Massasoit and Wampanoag history. In 1857, she mounted a legal battle to get paid for timber that had been taken from Native land. Today, Mitchell is remembered as a strong voice for Native heritage and rights.

Zerviah Gould
Mitchell

RECLAIMING A LOST LANGUAGE

When the Pilgrims arrived in New England, the Wampanoag people spoke their own language, called Wôpanâak (wom-pan-AH-ahk). But soon that language was under attack, part of a larger effort to erase Native culture.

As European settlers continued to establish colonies, they made it a goal to convert Native people to Christianity. The Wampanoag people had to conduct trade in English and send their children to English schools. There were even laws against using the Wampanoag language.

By the late 1800s, Wôpanâak was no longer spoken as a primary language. While certain words and phrases continued to be used, there were no fluent speakers of the language for more than 150 years.

But in 1993, a Wampanoag woman named Jessie Little Doe Baird decided that needed to change.

Jessie Little Doe Baird

She launched the Wôpanâak Language Reclamation Project so that the Wampanoag people could be fluent in their own language again. Baird enrolled in a graduate program at the Massachusetts Institute of Technology to study linguistics and language. She worked with other scholars, studying the Algonquin language and hundreds of colonial-era documents. They pulled together all those resources to create a dictionary with ten thousand Wampanoag words. Baird has continued to develop it and uses it as a resource to teach people of all ages.

Jessie Little Doe Baird's work earned her a celebrated MacArthur Genius Grant in 2010 and led to the creation of an immersion-style school where Wampanoag elementary school students can go to learn their language. Now, for the first time in six generations, there are fluent speakers of the Wôpanâak language once again.

Baird's work and her message, "We are still here," are efforts to counter the false story that Native people just disappeared after European colonization. Today's Wampanoag community includes people in Aquinnah, Mashpee, Herring Pond, Assonet, Pocasset, Pokanoket, Chappaquiddick, and Seekonk.

The original Wampanoag nation was much bigger than that. It was made up of sixty-nine villages throughout what is now southeastern Massachusetts, including Cape Cod and the islands of Martha's Vineyard and Nantucket, and eastern Rhode Island (east of Narragansett Bay). Due to the process of colonization, including diseases brought by Europeans, the Wampanoag people now have only those eight communities left.

Many older books say Native people didn't have a written language before European settlers arrived, but that's not actually true. Wampanoag people and other Native people did have written languages, but they were non-alphabetic. Algonquin people had a system of writing on birch bark. Wampum belts, made of beads from the quahog and other shells, had multiple purposes and served to communicate many different things.

SIX

LONG WINTER AT PLYMOUTH

When the Pilgrims finally landed after their long journey, they didn't see any people. Only trees. So where were all the Native people whose homes Champlain had drawn on his map? It's a sad story that also has to do with European travelers.

The Pilgrims weren't the first Europeans to visit the area we now call New England. French, Dutch, and English fishermen had been visiting for a hundred years, and when they came, they brought diseases that the Native people hadn't been exposed to. One of those diseases sparked an epidemic that spread through the region from 1616 to 1619.

That epidemic spread south from Maine, where the European fishermen had landed. Before 1616, the Wampanoag nation was made up of as many as a hundred thousand people in sixty-nine different communities. But the epidemic killed up to 90 percent of the Native people of the region. It wiped out entire villages, including the community of Patuxet, which was where Plymouth is now. That's why the Pilgrims arrived in 1620 to find cleared fields for farming but no people living there.

The Pilgrims should have been aware that Native people had lived in the area. They'd seen Champlain's map. But they either had forgotten about that or didn't want to talk about it. Instead, they wrote down details about the land they'd soon call home. Edward Winslow noted that the land had already been cleared for farming and that there was a sweet brook and springs of fresh water, a good harbor for ships, and excellent fishing. There was also a hill where they could build a platform for the colony's defense. It wasn't perfect, but it was going to be home, and the Pilgrims were grateful.

"*They fell upon their knees and blessed the God of Heaven who had brought them over the vast and furious ocean, and delivered them from all the perils and miseries thereof.*"

But the Pilgrims' perils and miseries were far from over. For starters, wintry weather had arrived by the time they dropped anchor in Plymouth Harbor. They were ready to settle in for the winter, but they didn't have anywhere to live. They'd been smooshed together on the *Mayflower* since early September. Now they'd finally arrived . . . and they *still* couldn't leave and spread out?

They had to live on the ship for several more months. They'd row to shore each morning and go to work building houses. Then they'd come back to the ship to sleep at night. It was a crowded, uncomfortable situation, made worse by the fact that everyone was getting sick. (About half of the original Pilgrims died that first winter.)

The Pilgrims starting building their homes in late December 1620 and finished the first house about two weeks later. It wasn't what anyone would call fancy, but at least it would be an improvement over living on the ship. The house was about twenty square feet and sat on the ground, with no foundation. Its walls were made of timber hewn from tree trunks, placed about two feet apart. Thin branches were inserted into holes drilled into the timbers to form a ladderlike structure. Clay was mixed with straw and then packed between the timbers, with the ladder structure to hold it in place. The Pilgrims called this construction method

Replicas of Pilgrim homes at Plimoth Plantation

"wattle and daub." They added an outside layer of boards to keep out the weather. Their new homes had thatched roofs, made out of reeds from the nearby marsh. There was no glass for windows. Instead, the Pilgrims covered the openings with used oiled parchment to let in a bit of light.

By March the Pilgrims were all ready to move off the ship and into their new homes, and in April the *Mayflower* set sail to go back to England.

WHAT DID PILGRIM HOMES LOOK LIKE INSIDE?

What exactly did the Pilgrims bring with them when they crossed the ocean to start new lives in Plymouth? They didn't leave behind a packing list, but we do have documents that show what kinds of possessions they had in their homes. When someone died, appraisers made something called a probate inventory—a list of all their stuff. Here's what Pilgrim Will Wright's home might have looked like inside, based on his probate inventory from 1633.

IN THE FIRST ROOM

- One chest with one sad colored suit and cloak
- One other suit, the breeches being without lining
- One red bay waistcoat and one white cotton waistcoat
- One old black stuff doublet, two hats—black and white
- Small table
- Carpet
- Cupboard
- Chair
- Six kettles, three iron pots, and a dripping pan
- Seven pewter platters, brass mortar and pestle, two pint pots, pewter candlestick
- Iron hooks
- Fowling piece
- Old blue coat
- Old flock bed, sheets, green rug

LOFT

IN THE LOFT OVER THE FIRST ROOM

- Half-headed bedstead
- Bag of feathers
- Old white rug
- Two hogsheads and a barrel

IN THE BEDCHAMBER

- One bedstead, one warming pan, one feather bed and bolster
- Two pillows with two rugs—one green and one white
- Trunk and little chair table
- Curtain and valance for the bed
- Tablecloths and napkins
- Two wrought silk caps, linen stockings
- One great Bible and a little Bible, one Greenham's works
- One psalm book
- Seventeen other small books

FIRST ROOM

BEDCHAMBER

BUTTERY

IN THE BUTTERY

- Two old barrels, one full of salt, the other half full
- Bucking tub
- Washing tub
- Two empty rundlets (small barrels) with small trifling things

IN THE LOFT OVER THE BEDCHAMBER

- One hog, one young sow of one year old, one shoat (young hog), one boar
- Two ewe goats and a ewe lamb
- One old sow
- One cow and steer calf

- One gouge
- Drawing knife
- Gimlet
- Two hammers
- Pair of old hinges, two chest locks, padlock
- Splitting knife
- Old spade
- Two old hoes
- Two fishing lines
- One old hogshead
- A churn
- Lumber

- Three iron wedges
- Garden rake, pitchfork
- One canoe
- Broadax, two felling axes, two handsaws

- Three augers, two chisels, thwart saw with wrest to it
- One small rundlet half full of powder
- Tiller of a whipsaw

It might seem strange to you to live in house that has only two chairs (and one of those is a weird combination table-chair!), but that was common in the time of the Pilgrims. Few people sat on chairs in Plymouth. Instead, they sat on benches, trunks, and chests—furniture that could do double duty by storing goods, too. Only important people in the colony had what were called "great chairs," which were more like our dining room or desk chairs today.

What a great chair!

The Pilgrims didn't have much to eat that winter. There had been no time to plant crops, so all they had was what they'd brought from England—hard biscuits, dried peas and beans, and salted fish and meat. So many people got sick that only about a half-dozen people were well enough to do all the chores and care for everyone else. By spring, the new colony's population had dwindled.

"But that which was most sad and lamentable was, that in two or three months' time half to their company died, especially in January and February, being the depth of winter, and wanting houses and other comforts; being infected with the scurvy and other diseases which this long voyage and their inaccommodate condition had brought upon them."

Translation: Half the people we brought over here died. January and February were the worst because it was so cold and nobody had houses and they were sick.

It was after that long winter, when their population had been cut in half, that the Pilgrims finally met the Native people in whose territory they had settled.

All winter long, the Pilgrims had seen smoke from their fires nearby. In February, they saw two Native men on a hill near the plantation and motioned for them to come over. Two Pilgrims started to walk toward them, but the Native men left. They'd spotted other Native people around the plantation, something that seemed to annoy Bradford, who wrote that the Indians kept "skulking about." One day that winter, the Pilgrim men went to dinner and found that their tools had been stolen while they were gone. (The Pilgrims were not as understanding about this as they had been when they were the ones taking the corn.)

Not long after that, a Native man came walking into the settlement. He spoke to the Pilgrims in English, and that was the beginning of a relationship that would change everything.

SEVEN

THE PILGRIMS AND THE WAMPANOAG PEOPLE

You might think that this is the part of the story where we talk about the first Thanksgiving. But that's still half a year away. First, the Pilgrims and Native people had to build a relationship.

The Native man who walked into Plymouth on March 16, 1621, started that process. His name was Samoset, and he was Abenaki, from Maine. He'd learned English from the fishermen who had visited there. The Pilgrims gave him some food, and he gave them some information. For starters, Samoset told them that the area where they'd landed was called

Patuxet. He also explained why they hadn't seen more Native people when they first arrived—because of that plague that had wiped out so many people four years earlier.

ABOUT THAT EPIDEMIC

Today, when disease sweeps through a community, scientists from groups like the World Health Organization and Centers for Disease Control and Prevention swoop in to find out what's going on and how to stop it. But in the 1600s, epidemics were far more likely to spread without anyone understanding what was causing people to get sick.

That was the case with the disease that killed so many Wampanoag people from 1616 to 1619. For a long time, all we knew was that the illness spread south from Maine, where European fishermen had made contact with Native people. But what was it?

We know some of the symptoms of this illness from historical documents.

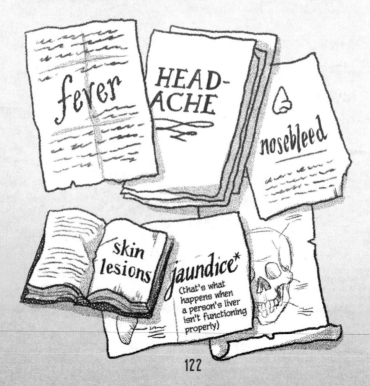

fever

HEAD-ACHE

nosebleed

skin lesions

jaundice*

(that's what happens when a person's liver isn't functioning properly)

Based on these symptoms, some historians guessed that the disease might have been yellow fever, smallpox, or plague. But it's a mystery that scientists have continued to wonder about. As time passes and we learn more about science, there are even more theories.

In 2010, researchers John S. Marr and John T. Cathey published a study suggesting a new idea—that maybe the Native people died of something called leptospirosis, complicated by Weil syndrome.

Leptospira is a group of bacteria that can cause many of the noted symptoms. When an infection is severe, it's called Weil syndrome and can result in liver and kidney failure and bleeding. We know today that *Leptospira* bacteria are carried by rats, which weren't native to America but would have arrived on the European ships. Infected rats could have contaminated the Wampanoag people's water, soil, and food.

We may never know for certain what caused

the epidemic, but the more researchers learn about infectious diseases, the closer they may get to solving the mystery. Paleomicrobiology is the study of microorganisms like bacteria in ancient remains, and every day, researchers who work in this field bring us closer to understanding epidemics from years gone by. It's one of the reasons that history—our understanding of the past—is always changing.

Samoset also told the Pilgrims why the Nauset people of Cape Cod didn't like the English (besides the fact that they stole corn).

"These people are ill affected towards the English, by reason of one Hunt, a master of a ship, who deceived the people, and got them under color of trucking with them, twenty out of this very place where we inhabit, and seven men from the Nausets, and carried them way, and sold them for slaves like a wretched man (for twenty pound a man) that cares not what mischief he doth for his profit." —FROM *MOURT'S RELATION*

Translation: Samoset said an English guy named Thomas Hunt came here a while ago, kidnapped more than two dozen Native men, and sold them into slavery.

So, no, the Nauset people didn't trust the English. And they had good reason not to. Hunt wasn't the only European explorer who had kidnapped Native people and sold them into slavery. There are records of several other explorers doing the same thing, including Captain John Smith, who had helped found Jamestown.

That same day, Samoset told the Pilgrims about

another Native man, named Tisquantum, who spoke even better English than he did. He also told them about Massasoit, the sachem of a village about forty miles away, with about sixty men.

After all that eating and conversation, it was getting dark, and that led to a bit of an awkward moment. Samoset wasn't showing any signs of getting ready to leave. The Pilgrims didn't know Samoset well. They didn't especially trust him, and he'd just explained that he didn't like English people because of that kidnapping jerk, Thomas Hunt. So what now?

"We would gladly have been rid of him at night, but he was not willing to go this night. Then we thought to carry him on shipboard, wherewith he was well content, and went into the shallop, but the wind was high and the water scant, that it could not return back. We lodged him that night at Stephen Hopkins' house, and watched him."

Translation: The Pilgrims wanted Samoset to go home. Samoset wanted to sleep over. They were going to let him stay on the ship, but it was too windy, so they put him at Stephen Hopkins's house instead.

The next day, Samoset went back to the village where Massasoit was sachem, but soon he returned to Plymouth with some other men. One of them was Tisquantum, or Squanto, as he'd come to be known by the English (possibly because they messed up his name). Tisquantum and his companions brought furs to trade and told the Pilgrims that Massasoit was nearby with his brother.

Sure enough, Massasoit showed up at the top of a nearby hill with sixty or so warriors. Tisquantum went to talk with him, then returned and said the Pilgrims should send someone to meet the sachem. Edward Winslow volunteered for the job. He put on armor and went with Tisquantum to see Massasoit. Winslow gave the Wampanoag men knives, copper chains, and biscuits. With Tisquantum translating, Winslow expressed that they'd like to be friends and allies. He told Massasoit that Governor Carver would like to talk with him to establish a formal peace.

That seemed like a good idea, but what if Massasoit went and discovered that he was walking into a trap? The two groups agreed to have Winslow stay with Massasoit's brother while Massasoit went with twenty of his men to meet with Carver and the other Pilgrims.

This wasn't the famous meeting we see in paintings of the so-called first Thanksgiving. It was actually a lot more important than that gathering because it was here that the Pilgrims and the Wampanoag people were able to work out an agreement of mutual protection. It had six parts.

1. That neither {Massasoit} nor any of his, should injure or do hurt to any of our people.

   Translation: Wampanoag men shouldn't hurt any of the Pilgrims.

2. And if any of his did hurt to any of ours, he should send the offender, that we might punish him.

   Translation: If any Wampanoag people hurt the Pilgrims, they'd be sent to be punished.

3. That if any of our tools were taken away when our people were at work, he should cause them to be restored, and if ours did any harm to any of his, we would do the like to them.

   Translation: If anybody steals anything, they have to give it back.

4. If any did unjustly war against him, we would aid him; if any did war against us, he should aid us.

   Translation: If either of our groups gets attacked, we'll have each other's backs.

5. *He should send to his neighbors confederates, to certify them of this, that they might not wrong us, but might be likewise comprised in the conditions of peace.*

Translation: The Wampanoag people should let neighboring tribes know about this deal to help keep the peace.

6. *That when their men came to us, they should leave their bows and arrows behind them, as we should do our pieces when we came to them.*

Translation: Wampanoag men shouldn't bring their weapons to meetings. And Pilgrim men shouldn't bring theirs, either.

The Pilgrims actually broke this agreement the same day it was made. After it was all worked out, Massasoit left, and his brother came to meet the Pilgrims. He followed the rules and left his bow and arrow behind. But he found that the Pilgrims were still carrying their guns. When he complained about this, the Pilgrims couldn't really argue. They put their muskets away.

When everyone else left, Tisquantum, or Squanto, stayed with the Pilgrims. They were happy to have his help because not only could he translate, but he also knew about foods they hadn't discovered yet.

"Squanto went at noon to fish for eels. At night he came home with as many as he could well lift in one hand, which our people were glad of. They were fat and sweet. He trod them out with his feet, and so caught them with his hands without any other instrument."

All that spring, Tisquantum stayed with the Pilgrims. He taught them to use herring from the brook to fertilize the soil when they were growing corn. He taught them the Wampanoag way of growing corn, beans, and squash, too—in mounds, where each plant helps the others grow better and produce more vegetables than if they were all planted in rows.

In addition to planting food that summer, the Pilgrims had hoped to grow stronger relationships with the Native people around Plymouth. They visited

Massasoit in his village in June and were a little surprised when they were invited to share a bed with him.

"He laid us on the bed with himself and his wife, they at the one end and we at the other, it being only planks laid a foot from the ground, and a thin mat upon them. Two more of his chief men, for want of room, pressed by and upon us, so that we were worse weary of our lodging than of our journey."

The following month, the Pilgrims were reminded that they had a debt to repay.

The relationship between the Pilgrims and the Wampanoag people was a complicated one, full of rumors and questions. Should they really trust one another? Tisquantum sometimes made things worse. Because he spoke both languages, he could play the two groups against each other. According to historical documents, he told people in other Native villages that the English kept the plague hidden away and could unleash it on them at any time. But, Tisquantum promised, if people paid tribute to him, he could keep the English from sending out their plague.

THE REAL DEAL ABOUT SQUANTO

If you've heard the name of one Native person who was part of the story of Plymouth, there's a good chance that name was Squanto. Maybe you learned that Squanto taught the Pilgrims how to grow corn at their new settlement. That

part of the story is true, but you probably haven't heard the real-deal details.

For starters, his name wasn't Squanto. It was Tisquantum, even though he shows up in all of the early Pilgrim documents as Squanto. We don't know why; it's possible the colonists heard his name wrong and made up their own spelling.

Tisquantum was in a special position to communicate with the Pilgrims because of an earlier experience with English explorers. Tisquantum was one of the Native men captured by Captain Thomas Hunt in 1614. Hunt's men had invited the Native men to their ship to trade. Then the explorers kidnapped them and took them back to Europe. Some were enslaved and sold in Spain. Tisquantum was sold to some other Englishmen and taken to England, where he was paraded through the streets so that people could see him, as if he were an animal on display in a zoo. He spent time enslaved in London and in Newfoundland, which is now part of Canada.

Through his whole ordeal, Tisquantum was learning to speak English. He was learning what the English men wanted and how to please them. In 1619, Tisquantum was brought back to America as a guide for another explorer, Thomas Dermer. When he went back to his old village, Patuxet—which is where Plymouth is located now—it was empty. Everyone who lived there had died in that epidemic. Can you imagine coming home after so many years away, only to learn that almost everyone you knew was gone?

Tisquantum continued traveling with Dermer, and in 1620, they were attacked by

Nauset men. Most of Dermer's men were killed. Dermer was wounded but escaped to Virginia. Tisquantum was taken prisoner by his fellow Wampanoags. They didn't trust him because he'd spent so much time with the English. But when more English people arrived that fall, the Wampanoag leaders decided that Tisquantum's ability to speak English might be handy. That's when they sent him to the Pilgrims, to serve as a guide and interpreter.

So Tisquantum, or Squanto, wasn't just a guy who offered to help out. He was a man who'd been taken captive twice in the previous few years—one who'd been sent to do a job that would help the Wampanoag people establish peace with the settlers.

In *Of Plymouth Plantation*, Bradford wrote that he believed Tisquantum had been sent to them by God.

"He directed them how to set their corn, where to take fish, and to procure other commodities, and was also their pilot to bring them to unknown places for their profit, and never left them till he died."

But Tisquantum had complicated relationships with both the Pilgrims and the Native communities. Even at the time, William Bradford realized that Tisquantum wasn't just there to help out.

"Squanto sought his own ends and played his own game, by putting the Indians in fear and drawing gifts from each of them to enrich himself, making them believe he could stir up war against whom he would, and make peace for whom he would."

Translation: Squanto was mostly interested in taking care of himself. He tried to make people afraid so they'd give him gifts and told them he was more powerful than he really was.

Most historians agree that when it came to relations between the Native people and the Pilgrims, Tisquantum played both sides. They also agree it's unlikely that the Pilgrims would have survived without him.

Despite all the rumors and mistrust, the shaky friendship between the Pilgrims and the Wampanoag people lasted through the summer. The bottom line was, the Pilgrims needed help learning to survive in this new place. And Massasoit was looking for allies. Because the Wampanoag people had lost so many of their villages to disease, the leaders of another tribe, the Narragansett, were pressuring Massasoit to join with them and pay tribute. Massasoit didn't want to do that, so he opted to make an alliance with the Pilgrims instead.

As the summer passed and the peace agreement held, the Pilgrims began to recover from their terrible, long winter. Their newly planted corn grew well. The barley and peas they'd brought from England? Not so much. But when September came, there was enough food that Governor William Bradford decided it was worth celebrating with a feast.

Finally!

We're going to talk about the first Thanksgiving *now*, right?

Well . . . kind of. But as usual, the true story was more complicated than the myth.

EIGHT
THE MYTH OF THE FIRST THANKSGIVING

One of the first things most American children learn about history is the story of the first Thanksgiving. You might remember hearing how the brave Pilgrims crossed the ocean to settle in Plymouth; how they survived a long, awful winter; and then how they sat down with Native people to celebrate the first Thanksgiving. This "first Thanksgiving" narrative is one of America's national origin myths—an inspiring tale that's become a symbol of the country's founding and values, even though the story isn't entirely true.

So what's the real deal about the first Thanksgiving? For starters, the 1621 autumn feast we like to talk about wasn't a "day of thanksgiving" for the Pilgrims. The Pilgrims did observe days of thanksgiving, but they weren't celebrations or feasts. They were days spent in prayer, giving thanks for something important. The Pilgrims actually held their first day of thanksgiving in Plymouth in 1623, when the colony saw some good rainfall after a long period of drought. They marked this thanksgiving in the traditional way—by spending it with morning and afternoon religious services, rather than partying with a lot of food.

Later, English settlers celebrated other days of thanksgiving. There's a good chance you've never heard of these other English days of thanksgiving, because they don't make for as nice a story as the 1621 feast. One happened in 1637, after the English had killed about seven hundred Pequot men, women, and children and burned their village, which was located in what is now called Connecticut. The English settlers held another special day of thanksgiving in 1676 to celebrate the death of Massasoit's son during King Philip's War (see p. 170). It's hard to reconcile these "thanksgivings" with paintings of the Pilgrims and Native people sitting down to dinner together.

What actually happened in the fall of 1621 was more of a harvest festival—something that was common in England and in other countries around the world. Wampanoag people had a long-standing tradition of harvest ceremonies, too. So the idea of giving thanks was nothing that the Pilgrims invented. And their harvest feast didn't happen in November, when America observes the holiday of Thanksgiving now. Documents suggest that the event we know as the first Thanksgiving actually took place in late September or early October, just after the crops were in. And everything we know about that event comes from one document. William Bradford never even talked about the celebration in his writings, though he did mention bringing in the harvest. *Mourt's Relation* includes the only real historical reference to the famous fall feast— and it never uses the words "harvest festival" *or* "thanksgiving."

"*Our harvest being gotten in, our governor sent four men on fowling, that so we might after a more special manner rejoice together, after we had gathered the fruit of our labors. They four in one day killed as much fowl as, with a little help beside, served the company almost a week. At which time, amongst other recreations, we exercised our arms, many of the Indians coming amongst us, and among the rest their great king Massasoit, with some ninety men, whom for three days we entertained and feasted, and they went out and killed five deer, which they brought to the plantation and bestowed on our governor, and upon the captain and others.*"

This is literally everything we know about the historic first thanksgiving. That Governor Bradford sent some men out to shoot fowl so they could have a feast after bringing in the harvest. That they killed a lot of ducks and geese. That they feasted and "exercised their arms," which probably refers to military drills that involved firing muskets. That Massasoit arrived with ninety Native men and joined the three-day feast. When they realized there wasn't going to be enough food, some of the Wampanoag men went out hunting and brought back five deer. So it turned into a sort of potluck harvest dinner.

The Pilgrims never referred to that meal as any sort of thanksgiving. In fact, no one would call it that for more than two hundred years.

It was 1841 when Alexander Young published a book called *Chronicles of the Pilgrim Fathers,* in which he included Winslow's notes about the harvest meal and decided that he'd call it "the first Thanksgiving."

When you think about Thanksgiving dinner, there's a good chance your imagined menu includes things like turkey, cranberry sauce, stuffing, and pumpkin pie.

But none of those foods are mentioned in the primary sources. Based on Winslow's writing, the only foods that we know were definitely part of that feast were venison and "fowl," which probably meant ducks and geese. We know from other historical documents that there were wild turkeys in the forests. Is it possible they were on the menu, too? Sure. But it's more likely that the Pilgrims' meal included fish, shellfish, and eels. (Try telling your family you'd like to have eels for Thanksgiving dinner this year, in honor of the Pilgrims, and let me know how that goes!)

We know that the Pilgrims had just brought in their harvest, so there's a good chance they ate some corn, beans, and squash at their feast. If the Native men brought their families, there might have been sopaheek, a stew made with corn and beans, with venison or other meat added, as well as squash or Jerusalem artichokes. Or perhaps they had nausamp, that porridge made from ground corn, with some nuts and berries added.

But many of America's traditional Thanksgiving foods would have been missing. There were cranberries in New England, but cranberry sauce wasn't a thing then. And there was no butter or flour to make crust, so pumpkin pie was also a no-go.

WHAT'S WRONG WITH THIS PICTURE?

Many paintings that portray the Pilgrims' first Thanksgiving show the myth, rather than a more accurate depiction. Based on what you've read about Pilgrims, the Wampanoag people, and the 1621 harvest celebration, how many inaccuracies can you find in this painting, which was done in 1914?

SIOUX HEADDRESS

Jennie Augusta Brownscombe,
The First Thanksgiving at Plymouth

For starters, the Pilgrims didn't live in log cabins like the one shown here. They also didn't dress in formal black-and-white clothes. And isn't the number of guests a little off? Remember that half the Pilgrims died during their first winter in Plymouth, so only fifty-three were left by the time this feast happened in autumn of 1621. According to Winslow's document, Massasoit brought ninety Native men when he showed up. Going by those numbers, there would have been twice as many Native people as Pilgrims at this feast. You wouldn't know that by looking at this painting, though.

Maybe you also noticed that the Native guests aren't dressed quite right. At least one of the Wampanoag men at the far end of the table is wearing a Plains-style headdress. The Sioux people were certainly around in 1621, but they lived out west, nowhere near Plymouth. Wampanoag men didn't wear headdresses like that, but because Sioux people were more often photographed and shown in magazines and early movies, many white people in the early 1900s expected all Native people to look like Sioux. That detail, along with the number of both groups of people at the feast, suggests that the artist may have been aiming to make a painting that white Americans would like, rather than one that was historically accurate.

So how did the September/October harvest feast that wasn't a real thanksgiving come to be celebrated by all of America on the fourth Thursday in November? It happened little by little. During the Revolutionary War, the colonists held an official day of thanksgiving to celebrate the victory of the Continental Army over the British Redcoats at Saratoga in 1777.

Surrender of General Burgoyne
by John Trumbull

That wasn't a turkey-and-pumpkin-pie situation yet, though. The push for an annual day of thanksgiving didn't get started until the mid-1800s, when Alexander Young published his book and decided he'd call the harvest feast "the first Thanksgiving."

The idea of Thanksgiving also got a big push from a woman named Sarah Josepha Hale, who became the editor of a popular magazine for ladies in 1837. She began a campaign to make Thanksgiving a national holiday.

She was pretty persistent about it, writing letters to governors and newspapers for more than a decade. By 1847, she was making a more specific argument—that America should recognize the last Thursday in November as Thanksgiving in every state.

Fast-forward now to 1863. Abraham Lincoln is president of the United States. The country is in the middle of the Civil War, families are being torn apart,

and people could use something to make them feel more unified. More like Americans. At a time when Abraham Lincoln was fighting to save the very idea of the United States of America, the story of the Pilgrims was a perfect symbol.

President Lincoln also declared two national days of thanksgiving for victories in battle, in 1862 and 1863. No one is sure how much attention Lincoln had been paying to Sarah Josepha Hale, but in 1863, he also declared a day of thanksgiving for the last Thursday in November, noting that the year had been filled with blessings and that even in the midst of a civil war, Americans should be thankful for peace and order.

There was still no promise that Thanksgiving would be a national holiday every year, even though almost every state had made it one by then. So Sarah Hale went back to sending letters, insisting that Thanksgiving should get its own day, just like Presidents' Day and Independence Day.

"Unless the President or the Governor of the State in office happens to see fit, no day is appointed for its observance. Is not this a state of things which calls for instant remedy? Should not our festival be assured to us by law?"

Translation: Somebody needs to make this official or we're never going to have a permanent Thanksgiving. Can we please fix this with a law or something?

Sarah Hale died in 1879, but her wish finally came true when Franklin Delano Roosevelt signed legislation to make Thanksgiving an official national holiday to be celebrated on the fourth Thursday of November, starting in 1942.

Again, America was at war—World War II, this time—and it's likely that the symbol of the Pilgrims seemed to be a good way to bring the country together.

PRIMARY SOURCES AND ANOTHER *MAYFLOWER* MYTH

The myth of the first Thanksgiving is a great example of how stories are embellished and changed over time until they don't look much like what really happened. A *Mayflower* story told by a famous suffragist—a woman who worked to get voting rights for women—is another great example of how primary sources can be helpful in figuring out the real deal about history.

In December 1893, Elizabeth Cady Stanton gave a talk at a fancy dinner in New York City. It was about Christmas on the *Mayflower,* and she described how the Pilgrims celebrated their first Christmas in their new home.

" . . . WHICH THEY WERE STRINGING FOR THE LITTLE INDIANS, AS THEY INTENDED TO INVITE A FEW OF THEM TO COME ON BOARD THE SHIP."

"THE MOTHERS HAD ALSO BROUGHT A BARREL FULL OF IVY, HOLLY, LAUREL, AND IMMORTELLES TO DECORATE THEIR LOG CABINS."

"OF THESE THEY MADE WREATHS TO ORNAMENT THE CHILDREN AND THE SALOON."

"AS SOON AS THE MAYFLOWER CAST ANCHOR, ELDER BREWSTER AND HIS INTERPRETER, AND AS MANY OF THE FATHERS AND MOTHERS AS THE LITTLE BOATS WOULD HOLD, WENT ASHORE TO MAKE ARRANGEMENTS ABOUT THEIR CABINS, TO VISIT THE SQUAWS AND INVITE THE CHILDREN."

"THE INTERPRETER EXPLAINED TO THEM THE SIGNIFICANCE OF CHRISTMAS, THE CUSTOM OF EXCHANGING GIFTS, ETC., AND THEY READILY ADAPTED TO THE INVITATION."

STANTON TOLD HER AUDIENCE THAT MASSASOIT WAS THERE, THAT HE CAME ON BOARD THE <u>MAYFLOWER</u> ON CHRISTMAS MORNING WITH TWO WOMEN AND SIX NATIVE CHILDREN, EACH CARRYING A SMALL BASKET WITH NUTS AND BERRIES TO GIVE TO THE ENGLISH CHILDREN.

158

STANTON TOLD THE LADIES THAT THE ENGLISH CHILDREN GAVE THEIR NEW NATIVE FRIENDS LITTLE TIN PAILS FULL OF TREATS, AND THAT THE PILGRIMS ASKED MASSASOIT TO STAY FOR DINNER, BUT HE SAID NO, BECAUSE HE WAS WORRIED THAT THE NATIVE CHILDREN DIDN'T KNOW THE RIGHT TABLE MANNERS.

THEN THE MOTHERS DECORATED THEIR TABLES AND SPREAD OUT A GRAND CHRISTMAS DINNER!

"AMONG OTHER THINGS, THEY HAD BROUGHT A BOX OF PLUM PUDDINGS."

BUT THAT'S NOT ALL. STANTON SAID THE FEAST ALSO INCLUDED GOOSEBERRY TARTS, BRUSSELS SPROUTS, SALT FISH, AND BACON—

A TRULY SUMPTUOUS DINNER.

♪ GOD SAVE ♪ THE KING . . .

"THEN THEY SANG . . . AND WENT ON DECK TO WATCH THE SUN GO DOWN AND THE MOON RISE IN ALL HER GLORY."

Elizabeth Cady Stanton's story was entertaining and full of vivid details. There was just one problem.

NONE OF IT WAS TRUE.

The Pilgrims didn't celebrate Christmas. They believed in only following the Bible, and there was nothing in there about celebrating Christmas Day. The Pilgrims thought that was a distraction from their real religion. So they didn't even exchange gifts with one another, much less introduce that custom to the Native children. Plymouth governor William Bradford made that super clear to some later non-religious settlers who dared to take Christmas Day off from work to celebrate in 1621. When Bradford got back from work that day and found them playing a game called stoolball in the streets, he took away their ball and bats. The Pilgrims were not big on Christmas fun.

Also, the Pilgrims hadn't brought along any sort of interpreter on the *Mayflower*. They didn't even meet Squanto or Massasoit until

the following spring. In December 1620, they barely had enough bug-infested biscuits left to survive the winter, so there was no "grand Christmas dinner." (And can you imagine eating brussels sprouts that had been packed in a ship with no refrigeration since September? That's gross, even if you loved brussels sprouts to begin with.)

Why would women's rights activist Elizabeth Cady Stanton tell such a made-up story? Here's a clue about how she might have been thinking about her audience. This is what she said to wrap up her talk to the ladies that day. . . .

THIS FRIENDLY RECEPTION, PLANNED BY THE FOREMOTHERS, MADE MASSASOIT AND HIS TRIBE STEADFAST FRIENDS OF THE LITTLE COLONY.

This is, of course, not really what happened between the Pilgrims and the Wampanoag people. But the story Elizabeth Cady Stanton invented made the point she intended—that Pilgrim *women* were the ones who had really made the whole thing work. That *women* were responsible for the success of America and ought to get more respect in society. This Christmas-on-the-*Mayflower* story probably inspired many in Elizabeth Cady Stanton's audience that day—women who were trying to be strong, independent leaders in the spirit of those brave Pilgrim ladies.

The real-deal story of what happened on the *Mayflower* on Christmas Day 1620 wouldn't have made for much of a dinner conversation. According to Edward Winslow's writings in *Mourt's Relation*, they went to shore that day and chopped down some trees for their houses. Then they went back to the *Mayflower*, had some beer, and went to bed.

NINE

FROM THE *MAYFLOWER* TO THE *SEAFLOWER*

Not everyone celebrates Thanksgiving, and that has a lot to do with the part of the Pilgrims' history that comes next. Not the myth of the first Thanksgiving, but the real story.

Not long after the Pilgrims arrived, it was apparent to the Wampanoag people that this group was different from the Europeans who had visited before. They were building houses, for starters. And they'd brought their families. They weren't going to fish for a while and go home to England. They were planning to stay.

Massasoit and his people decided that making peace with the newcomers was the best option. The

Wampanoag people had lost entire villages to the epidemic a few years earlier. An alliance with the English could help them if the Narragansett people attacked.

But soon it became clear that the newcomers didn't view the land the same way. In Wampanoag culture, the land was understood as a dish or bowl from which everyone could eat. In other words, the land took care of everyone. It wasn't viewed as anyone's "property." The Creator owned the land, so people couldn't own it, any more than they could own the water or the air. Wampanoag people believed in using the land according to the Creator's plan, so they had systems for land use. Family plots were distributed for homes and gardens and were usually given to women to manage.

The English settlers were more possessive about land. Specific parcels were owned by specific men (but not women—they wouldn't be able to own property in America for another two hundred years).

What's more, the English firmly believed that God wanted them to have the land where the Wampanoag people had lived for thousands of years. The English did purchase land from the Wampanoag people, and they kept records of those purchases. But there were

disputes because the two groups of people simply viewed land so differently. The Wampanoag people expected that they'd still be able to use the land's resources by hunting, fishing, and gathering things they needed. Meanwhile, the English built walls, and their livestock trampled the Native people's cornfields. English leaders kept pressuring the sachems, or anyone who would listen, to "sell" them more and more land.

By early 1622, there were signs that the peace between the Pilgrims and the Native people wouldn't last. The Narragansett people were upset about the alliance between the Pilgrims and Massasoit's people. The Narragansett sent a message to Plymouth—a bundle of arrows tied in a snakeskin. The Pilgrims' interpreters confirmed that this was not a welcome-to-the-neighborhood gesture, like showing up with brownies. It was a threat. The Pilgrims answered by sending the messengers back with a bunch of bullets wrapped in the same snakeskin. That March, they started building a wall around Plymouth. But that didn't solve anything, and the tensions continued.

By the winter of 1623, another English group, led by a man named Thomas Weston, had settled to the north of Plymouth in a place called Wessagusset, now known as Weymouth, Massachusetts. Tisquantum had died, so the Pilgrims had lost their main friend and interpreter, and there were rumors that Native people called the Massachusetts were going to attack Weston's settlement. In fact, Massasoit told the Pilgrims that the Massachusetts were planning to attack both Wessagussett *and* Plymouth, and that the only solution was for the English to attack first.

The Pilgrims sent a group, led by Myles Standish, to handle the situation. They warned Weston's men. Then they went to see the Massachusetts, pretending they wanted to trade with them. Instead, they killed two of the community's leaders, Wituwamat and Pecksuot, and some other men. They brought Wituwamat's head back to Plymouth and displayed it on a pole.

It probably doesn't surprise you that many Native people weren't interested in trading with the Pilgrims after that. But Massasoit was still loyal to the settlers and even came to William Bradford's wedding that August.

By 1630, more English ships had arrived, bringing a thousand men, women, and children to the Massachusetts Bay Colony, in what is now the Boston area. It

was clear to the Native people that these Englishmen were never planning to go home, and their presence was starting to change everything. The relative peace that had existed began to fall apart.

The English went to war with the Pequot people in 1637 after some attacks on English trading vessels. That year, the Narragansett people joined the English in attacking the Pequot. They set their village on fire and killed anyone who tried to escape. About seven hundred Pequot men, women, and children were killed. Plymouth governor William Bradford called it a "sweet sacrifice" and said his men "gave the praise thereof to God."

In 1642, a Narragansett sachem named Miantonomi visited the Montauk people on Long Island and asked them to join him in fighting the English.

He outlined a long list of reasons, explaining that while their ancestors always had plenty of animals to hunt, the English had ruined that by clearing the land and chopping down the trees. There was only one solution, he said. Force the settlers to go back to England. But the Narragansett-Montauk alliance never worked out. Meanwhile, the English colonies did come together. Plymouth, Massachusetts Bay, Connecticut, and New Haven joined to form the United Colonies of New England.

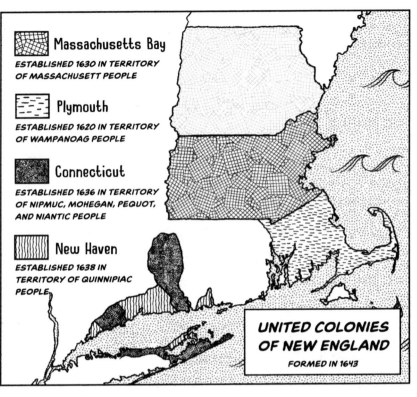

In 1657, William Bradford died. Massasoit died in 1661, and his son Wamsutta became the new sachem of Pokanoket. Around the same time, Wamsutta and Metacom, another of Massasoit's sons, asked to be given English names. From then on they were called Alexander and Philip in English documents.

More land disputes cropped up. At one point, Edward Winslow went to Pokanoket and brought Wamsutta to Plymouth at gunpoint. Wamsutta got sick on that trip and ended up dying. His brother accused Winslow of poisoning Wamsutta. When Metacom, who came to be called King Philip by the English, became sachem of Pokanoket, he never forgot what had happened to his brother.

Metacom began rallying other Native communities to join him in fighting the English, to force them back across the Atlantic for good. In June 1675, the Plymouth colonists executed three Wampanoag men who had been accused of killing a man. In response, Metacom and his men started attacking English settlements. This was the beginning of King Philip's War, which some historians consider to be the most brutal conflict in American history. At least 2,500 English colonists died, and more than twice as many Native people. Towns, villages, and supplies were destroyed. The war ended in 1676, not long after the English killed Metacom and enslaved his wife and nine-year-old son, along with many other Wampanoag people.

This is where another ship comes into the story—the *Seaflower*. It's not nearly as famous as the *Mayflower*. Instead of bringing hopeful Pilgrims to America, the *Seaflower* carried newly enslaved Native people to the Caribbean after King Philip's War. Ac-

cording to historical documents, it left Boston in 1676, bound for the Caribbean with a cargo of 180 Native men, women, and children. Plymouth governor Josiah Winslow (Edward Winslow's son) claimed that those men, women, and children were guilty of "many notorious and execrable murders, killings, and outrages" during King Philip's War. Their sentence? Slavery.

There's no historical record of exactly where they ended up. We know that their ship left for the Caribbean, but we also know that plantation owners there weren't excited to enslave people who had been involved in any sort of uprising.

RECONNECTING

Hundreds of years after the *Seaflower*'s voyage, Wampanoag people in New England have reconnected with the descendants of their ancestors who were shipped away and enslaved in Barbados and Bermuda. Now some Wampanoag people who live on St. David's Island in Bermuda travel to Massachusetts for the Mashpee Wampanoag Powwow each July. The Bermudan people have their own powwows, too, and some Wampanoag, Narragansett, and

The group brings the Bermudan tradition of Gombey dancing to the powwow.

Pequot people from New England attend those. Coming together to dance at powwows is one way they reclaim their culture, even as they remember all that was lost through colonization.

In the years that followed King Philip's War, Native people were robbed of their land, culture, and way of life. English, and later American, officials forced them off their land and into a system where they'd be taught to speak English and follow Christianity instead of their own languages, cultures, and religions. Many Native people view the arrival of the *Mayflower* in 1620 as the beginning of this process. For them, a holiday remembering the Pilgrims is nothing to celebrate.

"Thanksgiving is celebrated at the expense of Native Peoples who had to give up their lands and culture for America to become what it is today," said Linda Coombs, an Aquinnah Wampanoag historian and museum educator. She's one of many Native people and allies who choose not to celebrate this holiday.

In 1970, officials in New England were preparing a celebration to mark the 350th anniversary of the landing of the *Mayflower*. They thought it would be nice to invite Wampanoag people to share their reflections, too, so they asked Wamsutta Frank James, a member of the Aquinnah Wampanoag community and leader of United American Indians of New England, if he'd like to speak at their event. James accepted the invitation and wrote his speech. The people planning the event asked to see it in advance, so he showed them. They read it—and didn't like it. Perhaps they'd been expecting a happy talk about friendship and peace. Instead, they got the truth.

This is a time of celebration for you, celebrating an anniversary of a beginning for the white man in America. A time of looking back, of reflection. It is with a heavy heart that I look back upon what happened to my People. Even before the Pilgrims landed it was common practice for explorers to capture Indians, take them to Europe and sell them as slaves for 220 shillings apiece. The Pilgrims had hardly

explored the shores of Cape Cod for four days before they had robbed the graves of my ancestors and stolen their corn and beans. *Mourt's Relation* describes a searching party of sixteen men [who] took as much of the Indians' winter provisions as they were able to carry.

Massasoit, the great Sachem of the Wampanoag, knew these facts, yet he and his People welcomed and befriended the settlers of the Plymouth Plantation. Perhaps he did this because his Tribe had been depleted by an epidemic. Or his knowledge of the harsh oncoming winter was the reason for his peaceful acceptance of these acts. This action by Massasoit was perhaps our biggest mistake. We, the Wampanoag, welcomed you, the white man, with open arms, little knowing that it was the beginning of the end; that before fifty years were to pass, the Wampanoag would no longer be a free people.

Whatever the anniversary planners had been expecting, it wasn't this. They told James he had to change his talk. It was too inflammatory, they said. They wrote him a new talk—a *nicer* one—and told him he could deliver that speech instead.

Wamsutta Frank James said no. Instead of reading their words, he organized the first National Day of Mourning on Cole's Hill in Plymouth on Thanksgiving Day. Hundreds of Native people from tribes across the country joined him. There, he gave his speech the way he'd written it.

Although time has drained our culture, and our language is almost extinct, we the Wampanoags still walk the lands of Massachusetts. We may be fragmented, we may be confused. Many years have passed since we have been a people together. Our lands were invaded. We fought as hard to keep our land as you the whites did to take our land away from us. We were conquered, we became the American prisoners of war in many cases, and wards of the United States Government, until only recently.

Our spirit refuses to die. Yesterday we walked the woodland paths and sandy trails. Today we must walk the macadam highways

and roads. We are uniting. We're standing not in our wigwams but in your concrete tent. We stand tall and proud, and before too many moons pass we'll right the wrongs we have allowed to happen to us.

We forfeited our country. Our lands have fallen into the hands of the aggressor. We have allowed the white man to keep us on our knees. What has happened cannot be changed, but today we must work towards a more humane America, a more Indian America, where men and nature once again are important; where the Indian values of honor, truth, and brother-hood prevail.

Since that 1970 event, Native people and others have gathered in Plymouth each Thanksgiving to mark a National Day of Mourning. They protest the arrival of Europeans, honor their ancestors, and bring awareness to the issues that face Native people today. Always, they echo the message that Frank James delivered in 1970.

We are still here.

ABOUT THE FOOD
ON THE TABLE

Turkey, corn, squash, pumpkin, and cranberries are all indigenous foods that Wampanoag people hunted, cultivated, or gathered. Cranberries grew in wild bogs then, instead of being cultivated as they are today. The Wampanoag Tribe of Gay Head (Aquinnah) still has wild bogs on its tribal lands, and they still produce cranberries.

Today, families in America observe Thanksgiving in different ways. While some remember the Pilgrims, many choose to practice the more universal tradition of simply showing gratitude.

Gratitude has always been part of Wampanoag culture—not just with a once-in-a-while feast but as a part of everyday life. Throughout the generations, they've held celebrations like the Strawberry Thanksgiving and Green Corn Thanksgiving.

There were, and are, feasts to give thanks for other good fortune as well. These celebrations, called Nickommo, include Give-away ceremonies, in which people give away material things to show thanks to the Creator. The celebrations also feature food, music, dancing, and games. Nickommo are still a part of Wampanoag culture today.

AUTHOR'S NOTE

Like most Americans my age, I grew up learning the myth about the Pilgrims and the first Thanksgiving. As I got older, I began to hear other parts of the story—some of the real-deal details that don't make for such a pleasant school play production in November. And I remember being angry about that. Why couldn't kids learn the truth about history and hear all the different perspectives on what happened? Wouldn't that help us make better decisions and be better citizens? That's why I was excited to work on this series of books.

I was born in the year Wamsutta Frank James was invited—and then uninvited—to give his talk about the *Mayflower* anniversary. But I'd never heard his story until I was an adult. I'm grateful for the Native writers who have shared their perspectives, oral histories, stories, and research, especially Linda Coombs, Lisa Brooks, and Robin Wall Kimmerer.

Plimoth Plantation, a living-history museum where you can see what the colony may have looked like in its early years, was of great help in my research. The museum has reconstructed Pilgrim homes and furnishings, with reenactors playing the roles of real *Mayflower* passengers from the seventeenth century. Plimoth Plantation also includes a Wampanoag village, with wetuash, canoes, and modern Native people who share information about the lives of their ancestors, their culture, and the challenges Native people face in America today.

Plimoth Plantation opened to the public in 1957, but it's evolved over time. When the museum was created, it was based on historians' best guesses about history. As time went by, they realized they'd made mistakes here and there—building chimneys or making roof shingles out of the wrong material, for example—and so they made changes. As they studied probate inventories and other documents, they realized they'd put too much stuff in the houses. Pilgrims didn't own many things, so the museum staff scaled back.

They got rid of many of the beds, for example, when they realized that most kids slept on mattresses on the floor in those days.

The displays at Plimoth Plantation continue to change as we learn more about history. When I visited in the summer of 2018, there was a sign near the wall surrounding the Pilgrim village, explaining that it was unfinished and the staff was waiting for more information from a current archaeological dig before doing the rest of the work.

Plimoth Plantation's original mission statement never even mentioned the Wampanoag people who lived there. But in 1972, the people who ran the living history museum realized that was a mistake. That's when they started planning the Wampanoag Homesite, which would open at the museum the following year. Native people helped plan the project, and many took jobs working at the museum, hoping to educate visitors about Wampanoag people in an effort to unravel years of harmful stereotypes.

"We at Plimoth Plantation work very hard to peel away layers of inaccuracies and sift through centuries of misconceptions and misrepresentations," Linda Coombs wrote in the museum's magazine, *Plimoth*

Life. "Again, why is this important? Because to represent, by whatever means, any group as accurately as possible is to show respect. It shows respect for our people—both those of the past and those of today."

Pilgrim Hall Museum is also a wonderful resource for learning more about Plymouth. When I visited in August 2018, the museum had an excellent special exhibit called *Wampanoag World,* all about the culture and history of the Wampanoag people. The museum's permanent displays are also fascinating and were the source for many of the artifacts and paintings shared in this book.

Here are some other resources you might want to check out if you'd like to learn more about the Pilgrims and the Wampanoag people:

BOOKS

1621: A New Look at Thanksgiving by Catherine O'Neill Grace and Margaret M. Bruchac with Plimoth Plantation (National Geographic, 2004)

The Circle of Thanks: Native American Poems and Songs of Thanksgiving by Joseph Bruchac, illustrated by Murv Jacob (Bridgewater Books, 1996)

Mayflower *1620: A New Look at a Pilgrim Voyage* by Plimoth
   Plantation with Peter Arenstam, John Kemp, and
   Catherine O'Neill Grace (National Geographic, 2007)

Primary Source Detectives: Who Journeyed on the Mayflower?
   by Nicola Barber (Heinemann Library, 2014)

Samuel Eaton's Day: A Day in the Life of a Pilgrim Boy by
   Kate Waters, photographs by Russ Kendall (Scholastic,
   1993)

Sarah Morton's Day: A Day in the Life of a Pilgrim Girl by
   Kate Waters, photographs by Russ Kendall (Scholastic,
   1989)

*Tapenum's Day: A Wampanoag Indian Boy in Pilgrim
   Times* by Kate Waters, photographs by Russ Kendall
   (Scholastic, 1996)

WEBSITES

The General Society of Mayflower Descendants has a
website with information about *Mayflower* descendants
and genealogy resources.
themayflowersociety.org

The *Mayflower* History website is an extensive resource
created and maintained by historian Caleb Johnson.
mayflowerhistory.com

The living-history museum Plimoth Plantation has a website with information about visiting, as well as resources to learn more about the Pilgrims and the Wampanoag people.

plimoth.org

The modern-day Mashpee and Aquinnah Wampanoag communities both have websites with tribal news and information.

mashpeewampanoagtribe-nsn.gov
wampanoagtribe.org

Indian Country Today is a website with daily news about indigenous people throughout the Americas.
newsmaven.io/indiancountrytoday

The Wôpanâak Language Reclamation Project website has more information about efforts to bring back the Wampanoag language and includes a page with everyday English words that are derived from Wôpanâak.
wlrp.org/home.html

BIBLIOGRAPHY

Arenstam, Peter. "Perils of the Atlantic." *Plimoth Life* 9, no. 1 (2010): 2–4.

Avant, Joan Tavares. *People of the First Light: Wisdoms of a Mashpee Wampanoag Elder.* Joan Tavares Avant, 2010.

Baker, James W. *Thanksgiving: The Biography of an American Holiday.* Durham: University of New Hampshire Press, 2009.

Bradford, William. *Of Plymouth Plantation: 1620–1647.* New York: Alfred A. Knopf, 1952.

Bradford, William, and Edward Winslow. *Mourt's Relation; Or, Journal of the Plantation at Plymouth.* New York: Garrett Press, 1969.

Brooks, Lisa. *The Common Pot: The Recovery of Native Space in the Northeast.* Minneapolis: University of Minnesota Press, 2008.

Brooks, Lisa. *Our Beloved Kin: A New History of King Philip's War.* New Haven, CT: Yale University Press, 2018.

Coombs, Linda. "Holistic History: Including the Wampanoag." *Plimoth Life* 1, no. 2 (2002): 12–15.

Coombs, Linda. "Linda Coombs at the Pilgrim Monument and Provincetown Museum." Vimeo. October 2017. vimeo.com/240297766.

Curtin, Kathleen A. "Partakers of Our Plenty." *Plimoth Life* 1, no. 2 (2002): 4–11.

Deetz, James, and Patricia Scott Deetz. *The Times of Their Lives: Life, Love, and Death in Plymouth Colony.* New York: Anchor Books, 2000.

Delucia, Christine M. *Memory Lands: King Philip's War and the Place of Violence in the Northeast.* New Haven, CT: Yale University Press, 2018.

Dresser, Thomas. *The Wampanoag Tribe of Martha's Vineyard: Colonization to Recognition.* Charleston, SC: The History Press, 2011.

General Society of Mayflower Descendants. "Notable Descendants." themayflowersociety.org/the-pilgrims /notable-descendants. 2012–2017.

Hodgson, Godfrey. *A Great & Godly Adventure: The Pilgrims and the Myth of the First Thanksgiving.* New York: Public Affairs, 2006.

Johnson, Caleb. Mayflowerhistory.com. 1996–2017.

Kimmerer, Robin Wall. *Braiding Sweetgrass: Indigenous Wisdom, Scientific Knowledge, and the Teachings of Plants.* Minneapolis, MN: Milkweed Editions, 2013.

Langdon, George D. *Pilgrim Colony: A History of New Plymouth, 1620–1691.* New Haven, CT: Yale University Press, 1966.

Lipman, Andrew. *The Saltwater Frontier: Indians and the Contest for the American Coast.* New Haven, CT: Yale University Press, 2015.

Makepeace, Anne. *We Still Live Here* documentary, 2010.

Marr, John S., and John T. Cathey. "New Hypothesis for Cause of Epidemic Among Native Americans, New England, 1616–1619." *Emerging Infectious Diseases* 16, no. 2 (February 2010): 281–286. ncbi.nlm.nih.gov/pmc/articles/PMC2957993.

Mason, John. *A Brief History of the Pequot War.* Boston: S. Kneeland and T. Green, 1736. Accessed via DigitalCommons@University of Nebraska—Lincoln, digitalcommons.unl.edu/cgi/viewcontent.cgi?article=1042&context=etas.

Peirce, Ebenezer Weaver. *Indian History, Biography, and Genealogy: Pertaining to the Good Sachem Massasoit of the Wampanoag Tribe, and His Descendants.* North Abington, MA: Zerviah Gould Mitchell, 1878.

Peters, Paula. "Water Log: The Making of a Mishoon." *Plimoth Life* 9, no. 1 (2010): 18–19.

Peters, Paula, and Plimoth Plantation. "Tisquantum: The Real Story of Squanto." *Plimoth Life* 9, no. 1 (2010): 8–11.

Travers, Carolyn Freeman. "Fast and Thanksgiving Days of Plymouth Colony." *Plimoth Life* 1, no. 2 (2002): 16–19.

IMAGE CREDITS

INDEX

SMASH MORE STORIES!

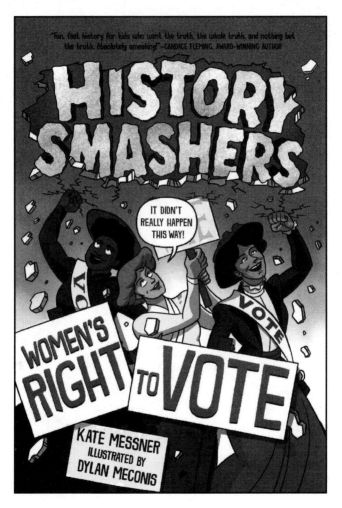

Turn the page for a sneak peek at the next book
in the History Smashers series!

You've probably heard stories about how American women won the right to vote. Chances are, you learned about Susan B. Anthony, who fought for that right along with some of her friends.

It's true that for a long time in America, only men could vote. That went on for more than a hundred years, until women got so angry that they did something about it. Maybe this is where you've imagined Susan B. Anthony and her pals coming into the story—a group of women in fancy hats, drinking tea, writing letters, and talking about equality. But that's just a tiny part of what happened.

The true story about women's right to vote is a lot longer and more complicated than that. And Susan B. Anthony was just a part of that bigger picture—a story of women who worked together but also fought with one another. They argued over everything from who should get to vote to how they should go about making change.

Sometimes those women had one another's backs, and sometimes they didn't. Some of the same white women who talked and wrote about justice and equality fought hard to keep women of color living separate and unequal lives. Sometimes the women who fought for voting rights were heroes—and sometimes not so much. Some of them worked hard to hide the contributions of other heroes because of the color of their skin. In the end, the story of women's fight for the right to vote is a much messier one than history books like to share. Let's smash that old story! Here's the real deal. . . .

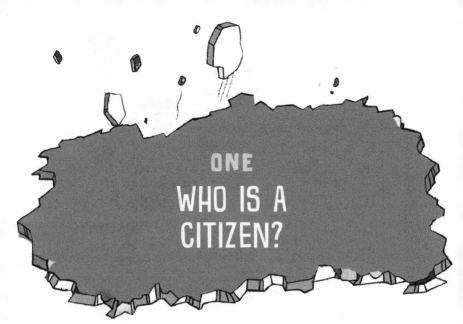

ONE
WHO IS A
CITIZEN?

Today it's hard to imagine how anyone could argue that some Americans should get to vote while others shouldn't. To understand the fight for voting rights, you have to understand that for the European men who colonized America, inequality was a tradition. Most of those early colonists came from England, where married women weren't even allowed to own property. Everything those women owned before they got married suddenly belonged to their husbands after the wedding.

In England, you had to be a man who owned property in order to vote. The colonists brought that system with them when they settled on the other side of the ocean. The men who wrote America's founding documents, the Declaration of Independence and the Constitution, held on to those old ideas when they set up the new nation's government. The only real discussion of women's rights at that time came from their wives.

As America was getting ready to declare its independence from Great Britain in 1776, Abigail Adams raised the issue in a letter to her husband, future-president John Adams.

In the new code of laws which I suppose it will be necessary for you to make, I desire you would remember the ladies and be more generous and favorable to them than your ancestors.

It's probably no surprise to you that John ignored Abigail's advice. Eleven years later, he and the other men in charge of the new nation sat down to write the US Constitution, the document that would outline how the government would work. They spent weeks debating what should be included, but they never even talked about the possibility of women voting. For the men in that room, that just wasn't how things worked.

Before the Revolutionary War, individual colonies had all kinds of different laws about who could vote and who couldn't. Sometimes it was based on race. In much of the South, where many Black people were enslaved, even free Black men weren't allowed to vote. You had to be male *and* white. Native American men were allowed to vote in some colonies but not others. And in some places, voting rights depended on religion.

When the colonies broke away from England, the new states made their own rules about who could vote.

Some decided to stick with tradition, giving the vote to men who owned a certain amount of property. Other states changed things up a little. In New Jersey, men could vote if they had *either* fifty pounds' worth of property or money. Vermont decided to let all men vote, whether they owned anything or not.

When it was time to figure out voting rights on the national level, the men who wrote the Constitution talked about including a property rule. Some lawmakers loved that idea. They were mostly from the South, where men who owned lots of property wanted to keep power for themselves. But others argued that men who didn't own property were already voting in some states. If the Constitution included a property requirement, they'd lose a right they already had. That didn't seem fair at all.

As the men talked, two very different ideas about voting emerged. Some said voting was **a privilege you should have to earn** . . . somehow. (Usually by having enough money to own property.) Others argued that voting was **a natural right** that should be given to all people, and that it couldn't—or shouldn't—be taken away by anyone.

The committee argued about this question for more than a week during the hot, sticky summer of 1787. Finally the men reached an agreement. They decided . . . not to make a decision. They left the issue of who gets to vote out of the Constitution entirely. The original document never mentions gender or property requirements. It only explains that under the new government, "people" would choose their representatives.

Not people who own property.

Not men.

Just people.

At first you might think that sounds great. There are no restrictions on voting in the Constitution! Everybody gets to vote! Right?

Wrong.

The way the Constitution is set up, everything that's *not* a national law is left up to the states. So when it came to voting rights, each state could decide who counted as a "person" in that state, and who got to vote. If your state decided you were person enough to vote in state elections, you could vote in national elections, too. If not, then you didn't get a say in how your country was run, either.

It probably won't surprise you to learn that wealthy white men counted as "people" in every state. Free Black men were most often considered "people" in the North but not in the South. And with the exception of New Jersey for a short time, women weren't "people" anywhere.

It turns out that the Constitution, the original set of rules for America's democracy, did little to make sure everyone would have a voice in the new government. In leaving the language so vague, the men who wrote the Constitution didn't really guarantee voting rights for anyone. Instead, they set the stage for battles that would rage on for decades . . . and that are still happening today.

HOW WOMEN VOTED IN NEW JERSEY . . . UNTIL THEY COULDN'T

When the new states set up laws about who could vote, women were banned from the polls *almost* everywhere. The one exception was New Jersey. There, the state constitution said "all inhabitants" of the colony could vote, as long as they were old enough and owned fifty pounds' worth of property. No one knows for sure why New Jersey didn't specify that only men could vote, as in the other states. Was it an accident? Or did the state mean for women to vote? There *were* lots of Quakers in New Jersey, and Quakers believe in the equality of all people.

Whatever the reason, women noticed the language in the state constitution. It didn't say they *couldn't* vote. So some of them showed up and voted. No one bothered them, and everything was fine for a while.

But as time passed, some men decided they didn't like the idea of women voting after all. They complained that the women who showed up at the polls weren't very ladylike. The men also had concerns about women getting too much power. What if they decided to vote all together on an issue? They could have a real influence on elections. So in 1807, New Jersey's lawmakers passed a law that said women couldn't vote anymore. Can you guess how many women had a say in that decision? None. All the lawmakers were men. With that vote, New Jersey's women lost their right to vote and didn't get it back for over a hundred years.